Patricia Zukowski, Editor

The Anthology Editorial Board:
Anne Bello
Andy Nicole Bowers
Thomas Hopper
Tommy Poehnelt
Benjamin Zender

The Student Writing Anthology

2015–2016

University of Massachusetts Amherst
Writing Program

HAYDEN
HM
McNEIL

Hayden-McNeil Sustainability

Hayden-McNeil's standard paper stock uses a minimum of 30% post-consumer waste. We offer higher % options by request, including a 100% recycled stock. Additionally, Hayden-McNeil Custom Digital provides authors with the opportunity to convert print products to a digital format. Hayden-McNeil is part of a larger sustainability initiative through Macmillan Higher Ed. Visit http://sustainability.macmillan.com to learn more.

Printed in the United States of America

10 9 8 7 6 5 4 3 2 1

ISBN 978-0-7380-8026-0

Hayden-McNeil Publishing
14903 Pilot Drive
Plymouth, MI 48170
www.hmpublishing.com

Hoang 8026-0 F15-S

Table of Contents

Part 1: Essays from *Basic Writing*
Prefaces and Introductions by Anne Bello

Part 2: Essays from *College Writing*
Prefaces and Introductions by Patricia Zukowski

Writer's Statement

Introduction

Since 1982, the Writing Program has worked from the core belief that undergraduate students are immersed in a rich print and digital culture and that they are *already writers* whose ideas are worth sharing, crafting, and revising into prose that should be read. This 38th edition of the UMass Amherst *Student Writing Anthology* maintains our longstanding respect for student writing by publishing select essays written for first-year writing classes primarily during the spring and fall semesters of 2013 and spring semester of 2014. The book serves as an essential learning and teaching tool in both our *Basic* and *College Writing* courses, praised for its value by students and teachers alike. It also fulfills the critical goal of helping these texts to circulate among a wider readership.

We invite our readers to contemplate the vital issues and original thinking in these essays, and for those who are reading *as writers*, to also consider the effects of each author's rhetorical choices. Part 1 begins with essays selected from each of the four units of *Basic Writing*—a reading- and writing-intensive course that explores issues of U.S. diversity. Its students read and write about physical, national, linguistic, and cultural borders that shape life in the United States. The excellent writing from this course asks us to consider how culture and identity interact, reinforcing some borders and blurring others. Understanding how societies differ and valuing cultural difference—including different forms of communication—are essential educational experiences for us all.

Part 2, devoted to *College Writing*, illustrates the goals of that course: to write with purpose and power, to develop one's ideas critically, and to effectively tailor one's prose to a specific audience. In this course, students are asked to explore topics that are personally meaningful and to write about these topics to readers who *need* to engage with these ideas. In these essays, readers will find that students are not only writing to our university community, but also translating the thinking and research valued in the academy to a broader public. This section begins with essays from three of the course's five units: "Inquiring into Self," "Interacting with Text," and "Adding to the Conversation." Our fourth unit is called the "TBA" because each of our teachers designs a unique project. While these assignments build on goals and concepts covered in the first three units of the course, we have not included essays from this unit since each project is specific to each class. The section concludes with the final essay assignment, the "Writer's Statement." Throughout the course, students reflect on various aspects of their drafting, revision process, and the final product of their work. In "Writer's Statement," students look back over the whole body of work they have produced in the course, consider their struggles and successes, then synthesize into one paper what they believe are the most salient lessons they will carry with them from the course. These papers offer sound and insightful advice to any writer.

We welcome readers to discover the many rhetorical choices available to us in academic writing and to learn from the wealth of ideas and experiences that emerge from each writer's personal context. Finally, we hope our readers will enjoy the excellent work produced by UMass Amherst students.

Acknowledgments

I am grateful to so many people who made this book possible: the First Year Writing instructors who nominated their students' excellent texts for possible inclusion in the *Anthology* (far too many names to recognize here), and all the students who so eagerly agreed to share their work so that others might learn from it. However, not one step of this process would have gone forward without the extremely competent, dedicated, and enthusiastic work of our office assistant, Jillian Sacco. An undergraduate, Jillian's work was key in every aspect of producing this book and was as professional as any permanent staff member of the program. Needless to say, she succeeded in her efforts on all fronts. I also wish to thank two of our graduate student instructors, Korka Sall and Ann Ward, for their contributions in preparing the manuscript. Korka and Ann assisted me in fact-checking citations and shared the role of being my second readers in editing the *College Writing* essays. Our new publisher, Hayden-McNeil, also deserves recognition for making our transition to their company as smooth as possible and for their attentive and creative design work on the book.

***

The efforts of our *College Writing* Anthology Committee members were extraordinary. Every week throughout the fall 2014 semester, they received a batch of 15–25 papers, read them intensively and attentively, then scored and commented on each one. The committee met every Friday afternoon to thoughtfully, thoroughly, and spiritedly discuss each text for consideration that week. Four volunteer graduate student committee members—Andy Nicole Bowers, Thomas Hopper, Tommy Poehnelt, and Benjamin Zender—showed graciousness and dedication throughout the entire process. We were also privileged to have Anne Bello, Deputy Director of the Writing Program, participate as a full committee member in every meeting. The work she contributed was invaluable. Not only did she offer critical insights on every *College Writing* submission; she also created the entire *Basic Writing* section of the book. Once she and graduate student instructor Florianne Jimenez selected, themed, and organized the *Basic Writing* essays included in the book, Anne edited them and wrote all the prefaces and essay introductions for the *Basic Writing* section. She also offered invaluable advice and support to the editor throughout the many steps that go into developing a new text. Finally, we all owe a great debt of gratitude to our Writing Program director, Haivan Hoang, for her commitment to the principles behind this project and the many ways she has supported the development of this book. Through these efforts of so many dedicated members of the Writing Program, all our first-year students and teachers have access to this valuable learning resource—a required text in both *Basic* and *College Writing*.

Patricia Zukowski
Chair, Anthology Committee

Part 1

Essays from *Basic Writing*

Speaking for Oneself:
Colliding Spaces

Preface

What is a border? Students in *Basic Writing* (Englwrit 111) are invited to consider this seemingly simple question early in the semester. Answers often come quickly and easily—at first. A border is an edge, a boundary, a space where one thing ends and another begins. A border would seem to be the very definition of something that is clear cut.

But as the essays that follow show, borders can be far more complicated than they initially appear. In the first unit of the course, students read about borders in a number of contexts, from cities to airports to the online world. Through reading, writing, and discussion, students complicate their initial ideas about borders, realizing that borders can be intangible concepts as well as physical spaces. Students then write an essay that asks them to reflect upon their own experiences crossing (or not crossing) borders. By critically examining their own experiences, students begin to realize that "borders shape everyone differently," as Yongyan Cai explains in her essay, "A Disappeared Border." Borders can be barriers that isolate or protect, or they can be places for crossing and exchange. Sometimes borders exist only in our minds, as Eric Zhang claims in his essay, "Am I 'White Wash'?": "The border that is blocking me from being who I want to be is just an imaginary border." Jessica Mazzola, however, argues that some borders are defined by their permanence, even if they are intangible. She writes that her "shyness can be considered a border because even if it is mostly assumed to be fixable, it's always been a part of me." As students' understandings of borders deepen, they begin to pose questions about identity and culture that they explore throughout the other units of the course.

A Disappeared Border

YONGYAN CAI

Cai begins her essay by focusing on a literal border crossing: the experience of flying from China to the United States. Using narrative and purposefully selected details, she describes the different tangible and intangible borders she has crossed by coming to the United States to study.

This story started three years ago. In a city located in the south part of China, which was still in burning hot summer, people never got bored of going out to enjoy the warmth of the sun. Meanwhile, a city on the East Coast of the United States was ready to meet the winter, and I was on my way to this strange city.

I fought back tears, but eventually I had to drag my giant suitcases and leave the city and country I had lived in for sixteen years. I didn't have any communication with my parents on the way to the airport, but I could see the pride on their faces. I tried not to recall anything about this familiar city or any memory that would induce me to regret my decision of going to the United States. Because of the early morning departure of my flight, we had to leave home one day prior to my departure date. But without any specific reason, discomforts came to me successively, which made me feel the time going by extremely fast.

In the airport, sparsely populated in the early morning, a few people were drinking coffee leisurely. It was time to go. We stood in front of the security entrance, and I tried very hard to avoid looking at the red rims of my mother's eyes. My father couldn't hide his satisfaction since he had never thought before that his only daughter would have the chance to go to the United States to study. My ruefulness came up immediately when I saw my mother's eyes, so I pushed my parents away quickly and walked into the security entrance directly. I didn't turn around and look back at my parents until I made sure that I could only see their faces vaguely. When I arrived at the boarding gate, the broadcast was repeating: "Passengers who are taking Flight 380 from

Hong Kong to New York, we are boarding now. Please have your boarding pass and identification ready."

I found my seat and noticed that the boy sitting next to me was also a student. He was going to the same city for his second year in the United States.

There was no trace of sadness on his face, and it even seemed like he was going home instead of leaving. I kept wondering whether I would be like him in one year. And suddenly, one of my brothers popped into my mind. He is not my biological brother, but he treats me as his real sister. He lived in Canada for five years and had never visited home since he arrived there. I asked him for reasons, and he explained that he just hated the terribly awful feeling of choking back tears while saying goodbye to his parents in the airport.

After an almost 14-hour flight, I arrived in New York's JFK Airport. It was hard to believe that an airplane took me across the border from China to the United States by stepping over oceans and countries. It leads me to wonder if a border is really that easy to cross. I took the air train to the boarding gate, and I looked around at the people surrounding me who came from different countries. They did not look troubled by the sad feeling caused by leaving home, and I seemed like the only outsider. In JFK, there were foods from various countries in the food court, which helped people have more sense of belonging. But it did not work on me because it was not real Chinese food. In the essay "Where Worlds Collide," Pico Iyer points out that an airport is just like a huge melting pot mixed by every little thing from all over the world: "And in their very universality—like the mall, the motel, or the McDonald's outlet—they advance the notion of a future in which all the world's a multi-culture" (18). For me, airports are miraculous and incredible places, and we are not able to predict what will happen next. Just like Iyer writes, "The deeper drama of any airport is that it features a kind of interaction almost unique in our lives, wherein many of us do not know whom we are going to meet or whom others are going to meet in us" (24). There are countless people separated from their families and left alone. Also, there are innumerable people who kiss and say goodbye to loved ones. An airport could be seen as a home: people sleep here, take showers here, and eat here. An airport could also feel like a tiny world, a place where people all around the world come and leave from. Airports enable us to step over oceans toward other oceans, from countries to other countries.

I felt cold, and I immediately felt like there was no hot water in New York, maybe even in the United States. I saw many people sitting in the corner covering their weeping faces with their hands and talking on the phone. Suddenly, the boy I met on the plane and the brother I had remembered came to my mind. Had they done the same things as these people did in the airport? Would I behave like one of them?

The answer is no. Borders shape everyone differently. During this whole year, an airport has been not only a huge border that separates me from my homeland but also an invisible boundary that has stayed in my mind. Every time in the Hong Kong airport, even though I was not leaving yet, I felt I was not part of my country. When I arrived in Boston, the airport always made me feel that I didn't belong there. Nonetheless, I never thought about this situation before. This intangible border I built up in my mind truly disappeared without a trace after one year. Boston was becoming a place like home to me after one year passed. Home is a place giving you comforts and bringing your mind peace. Home is also a place arousing boundless hope about the future. Boston is the exact city like that for me. I was not an outstanding child who could always achieve impressive grades at school but one who always disappointed her parents, even let them feel hopeless. They decided not to attend the parents' meeting because they felt ashamed of me. Nevertheless, after I came to the United States, everything changed incredibly. I saw an "inconceivable" expression and pride on their faces for the first time. It was also the first time that I had seen them too impatient to tell others that their daughter was studying in the United States. And my father never said things like this before: *You have no idea what tremendous and infinite potential you have.* Boston was no longer the place that made me feel homesick or sad but was instead the place that guided and encouraged me to believe in and explore myself more deeply.

After this whole year, I still miss my hometown, but thinking of the word "border," I feel I have moved beyond that. I feel I completely started from scratch with a brand new self; I am becoming a better person. When I think back to the little girl who always disappointed her parents, I realize I did something that I never imagined and became someone who I never thought I would be. Sometimes when you see a border stand in front of you, just try to face it before you escape and maybe you will earn something beyond what you thought. In the beginning, the border was hard to cross. But when I crossed it, I got through hardships and dug out more than I expected from inside of myself. I still count the days until summer and Christmas holidays. But every time those days come, I realize that I do not eagerly want to leave here as I expected, and I know I am going to miss this place a lot. The border is no longer there because this place is my home.

Work Cited

Iyer, Pico. "Where Worlds Collide." *Reading and Writing on the Edge*. Eds. Deirdre Vinyard et al. Boston: Pearson, 2014. 16–29. Print. Mercury Reader Ser.

Shy

JESSICA MAZZOLA

Mazzola explains how shyness functions as a border in her life by describing her experiences in a specific context: the classroom. By analyzing her personal experience, Mazzola illustrates how borders can protect and define as well as separate and isolate.

I was trying to talk to my teacher. There were too many background voices and noises, so I risked speaking louder than I usually do for her to hear me. Just my luck, everyone paused in speech the minute I started. When I felt the room look at me, I silenced myself and shrank in my seat from embarrassment, waiting for the moment to pass. It feels like my heart literally shrinks in size every time this happens; I can no longer speak and all I want to do is disappear.

This and many similar experiences like it have plagued me for as long as I can remember. I'm not sure why I'm so shy, but to me it feels like an invisible border, blocking me from many different opportunities I could've obtained. Whenever I experience it, I feel trapped in. I can't make myself be heard or seen. It's like a fail-safe boundary I've built for myself so that I won't get made fun of or get embarrassed by whatever I could say. I feel kind of negatively towards this. I believe certain things require more confidence and independence in order to achieve more success. However, I also don't feel that badly towards it because it's how I avoid being noticed by people who could hurt me in response to any confidence I reveal.

I used to sit farther away from the front of the room, and this introduced a conflict. What if I needed to ask a question? I didn't want to go right out and ask for fear of it sounding silly in addition to everyone noticing me. In the past, I'd felt victimized and embarrassed from this kind of situation; I knew how it played out. I'd raise my solitary hand to ask a question, and when I'd get picked I'd ask my question, only to be asked to speak louder. I'd start to feel warm when I spoke loud enough for all to hear, and it would become worse when I realized I had just missed what the teacher already said. Conclusively, I would be both noticed and singled out as not very bright. My face would flush red and once again I'd shrink in my seat waiting for invisibility to cloak me from the prying stares of my classmates. This instance is also representative of my boundary because I can't ask the questions I need to understand important concepts. I always try to figure out a path around this obstacle, but the truth is I'd probably be way better off by being direct.

To me these experiences are sound representations of my border. I chose classroom experiences because they are where I have encountered my border the most. They are also where the encounters have been the most memorable. When you have been with a group of people since elementary school, and everyone has made their friends, it's difficult to show much of yourself without being judged. Some people are relatively nice but they won't look to you for a friend, so you do not do the same in return. I did not have a lot of friends in school, but I was okay with that because the ones I had were all very close. However, because of this, I had all these situations where I was surrounded by people I did not know well. Thus, I had no motivation to be outgoing or to express myself, and of course I wasn't going to even if there was motivation.

These experiences I've had are especially significant because my shyness is one of the sole parts of me that I fully understand. I understand how it works into my everyday behavior and how that behavior comes back to affect me. A little shyness every once in a while in certain situations is okay, but having it pop up all the time in social situations or in a classroom is not okay. In a classroom, I won't be able to understand the material as well if I don't suck it up and ask questions. In a social situation, I won't be very skilled at making good friends and interacting with them. This is my border, and every time I come across a situation where I am singled out, I feel it stop me from expressing myself as a way of protection, as a block.

I feel that shyness can be considered a border because even if it is mostly assumed to be fixable, it's always been a part of me. In my eyes, it's never going to go away. Shyness is always going to be present when I'm in a social situation. It prevents me from going that extra length to be outgoing, to interact, and to ask questions. In truth, I feel that I can lessen this quality and make it less prominent so that I won't be as in the dark. I won't have as big of an obstacle blocking me from the successes I could gain in my life. However, overall I do not feel that I can completely just make it disappear. In my eyes, I can't completely cross this border.

Am I "White Wash"?

ERIC ZHANG

Zhang poses powerful questions about racial and cultural identity by reflecting upon his understanding of the term "white wash." The invisible borders Zhang identifies—and wrestles with—in this essay foreshadow some of the key questions about culture and identity explored in Units 2, 3, and 4.

"Hey Eric, do you watch anime?"

"Hey Eric, where were you born? Were you born in China?"

"Hey Eric, I bet you have straight A's in all of your classes."

There are days where I just want someone to ask me anything that is not related to something "Asian." But I also can't have a life where people think I am from China. I have studied people time in and time out on their facial expressions, and almost every time they give me the same face of surprise when I say I was born in Massachusetts. They would be like, "Oh really?!" like I was out of this world. To be honest, I sometimes like it when people find out that I am an American so that way when people ask me something about China, I can say I never visited. However, sometimes that can be bad. When they think I don't know anything about China, they think I am a white wash: an Asian who truly does not know a single thing about his home country.

My Asian friends make fun of me for being the so-called term "white wash" because I don't watch the same anime they do or know the new music from Korea. They think I dropped all the knowledge I have about my culture and turned completely white. But how can I not? America in my eyes is about being who I am, not what people say I can or can't be. It's like going to college and especially coming to UMass: I can be whoever I want and no one should bat an eye.

Now I'm not saying I don't know anything about China. I do have some knowledge, but thanks to the public schools I was taught the life of an American. My two conflicting cultures create an invisible border where if I cross into one I would have to completely give up on the other. Non-Asian people would just use the word "white wash" like it's nothing, but as someone who is trying to keep in touch with my culture, it's really hard for me to not yell at them when they say it. People would throw that term out loosely and arguments would fly. (When I hang out with my Asian friends, we don't talk about issues that might be going on in our home countries. When I hang out with them, they don't have any problems talking about their lives, and I don't either; we help each other when we really need the help.)

Last week I was hanging out with some of my American friends, and some-how we came across the topic of what really defines the meaning of "white wash."

"No, I don't think I am white wash," I said.

"Ah no, Eric, the way you have been acting for the past year, you are by far the most white Asian I have seen," my friend said.

"Acting 'white' doesn't mean I am white wash. Being born here makes me American. My skin color doesn't define how I should act."

"So what really is a white wash Asian then?"

"If you are born in America and your *background* is Asian, and if you decide to embrace your family culture, I'm sure your parents would be proud. But if you want to have an American lifestyle, then it's your choice. HOWEVER, if you are born in an Asian country and move to the US and then completely drop everything you know about your culture, then that is when you are white wash."

I sat there afterwards thinking about that statement. Is that something a white wash Asian would say just to hide the truth? I don't think so. The border that is blocking me from being who I want to be is just an imaginary border; there is no problem with my situation. Being white wash is just something someone would say to an Asian if they think that person is not acting like the stereo-typical Asian they would see on TV (though sometimes I make fun of the stereotypes by acting them out just because it's really funny). When I came to UMass, most of the people from my dorm thought that I was from another country, but I soon let them know that I'm American. I like the American way of life, but don't take me as someone who doesn't know a single thing about my culture because I do.

Speaking to Respond and Engage:
Defining Lines, Unsettled Voices, and Interweavings

Preface

After critically examining their own experiences with borders in Unit 1, students read and write about specific contexts in which borders shape identity and culture. In the Defining Lines unit, students explore questions of immigration and assimilation, and in the Unsettled Voices unit, students examine how languages can create, reflect, and reinforce connections and divisions between groups of people. The Interweavings unit looks at how cultures can flow across borders and how individual identities evolve in multilayered spaces. For each unit, students write a different type of essay: an in-depth response to a single text, a rhetorical analysis, and an argument incorporating multiple texts.

The essays that follow demonstrate the range of approaches students take to unit assignments. Hind Aljarahi, Jennifer Ochaeta, and Jiaqi Wei offer sustained responses to single texts, while Kudzai Chidarikire, Doreen Frimpong-Brago, and Michael Mascio weave together multiple sources. Though all of these writers crafted their essays within the context of *Basic Writing*, their texts articulate different purposes for writing. Frimpong-Brago, for example, explains that reading and writing became part of an "attempt to find answers to some of [the] questions" she had about her own identity. Aljarahi, on the other hand, states she hopes "that through reading this essay, people can look at this problem differently" while arguing for improving conditions for undocumented immigrants.

These writers respond and reflect, synthesize and engage. Wei concludes her essay, a cross-cultural examination of language-based social prejudice, by asking readers to challenge their beliefs about multilingual immigrants: "So will you change your attitude to this part of mainstream population?" Her essay— like all of the essays that follow—invites readers to engage with complex questions of culture and identity. As Chidarikire so aptly explains, "The very idea of identity is a complicated matter in itself; some people spend their entire lives trying to discover who they are." Chidarikire then adds that considering culture as well further complicates these ideas. Drawing on their knowledge of different texts, different cultures, and even different languages, these writers grapple with questions personal and global, political and philosophical. Their essays serve both as representations of the fine writing done in *Basic Writing* and as invitations for readers to join in the intellectual work of the course.

Undocumented

HIND ALJARAHI

Aljarahi's essay illustrates one way writers can respond to a text without directly sharing personal experiences with the author. Her essay also demonstrates how writers can combine summary and response to put forth their own ideas.

Citizenship is a title that can literally change lives, yet many of us don't appreciate the grace and luxury we have as citizens. Being able to work, go to school, travel, and have a healthcare provider are just a few of the many necessities that undocumented immigrants are unable to enjoy. Reading Jose Antonio Vargas's essay "My Life as an Undocumented Immigrant," I was immediately reminded of my own friend, Mila, and her struggle trying to hide her identity as an undocumented immigrant. Reading the essay, I realized how Mila and Vargas have similar battles and have both gone through extensive amounts of agony in the process of hiding their identity.

As he explains in his essay, Vargas was born in the Philippines and was sent to live in the U.S with his grandfather, Lolo, when he was only 12 years old. He grew up thinking that he was a legal citizen of the U.S until he attempted to obtain his driver's license. The D.M.V informed him that his green card was fake. This was shocking to him especially when he knew nothing about this and was truly at a loss finding out about it. After Vargas found out about being undocumented, he was determined to become successful, and that helped him stand out compared to his fellow classmates. With the aid of his school officials, Pat Hyland and Rich Fischer, who both found out about his situation, he was able to attend San Francisco State University on a full ride.

Although Vargas's determination and hard work paid off, the fact that he was undocumented did not change. Vargas still had to hide his identity from those around him even after becoming a successful journalist. Vargas faced many difficulties in his life and had to overcome many challenges. Once he became a well-known journalist, he decided that he could not run away forever because nothing would ever change that way. He couldn't be a successful journalist lying to people about his own identity. He wanted change and for change to happen, he needed to tell the world about his story and get the support he and other undocumented immigrants need. Someone needs to speak up in order for their voice to be heard and for change to happen.

Reading about Vargas's experiences made me think about my friend, Mila. The first time I met Mila was during my sophomore year of high school. I remember sitting in class as Mrs. Nottingham introduced her to everyone. "This is Mila everyone," she said. "She is from Italy, and she will be joining us this semester." The next day, I decided to sit next to Mila. I introduced myself, and since she had arrived halfway through the year, I offered her my notes. As the days passed, we became very close. We studied together, went out together, and attended events together. Mila is not only extremely intelligent but also exceptionally responsible. She took care of her little brother every other day after school. She never had a grade lower than an A— and was simply on top of everything. When senior year of high school came, she was working 43 hours a week, which would be considered full-time! She gave some of the money she made to her parents and the rest she saved.

It was our senior year of high school when I found out that she was an undocumented immigrant. I remember asking her where she wanted to go and what she wanted to study. She looked at me and said, "Hind, I don't think I can attend college." I was in shock and wanted to find out why, but I did not ask anything else. I was hoping that she would tell me herself. I did not ask her because I did not want her to tell me something that she was not ready to convey. Eventually, she decided it was time for me to know her secret. She gathered up all of her courage and told me everything. I wasn't in shock when she told me. I felt like I knew all along. It was as if I knew but was waiting for her to open up to me. Being her friend afterward did not feel any different. We continued doing all the things that we did together the exact same way. If anything, it brought us closer. The only thing that was different was that I had the urge to help my friend who was in need of support and guidance.

Vargas's and Mila's struggles are similar in several ways, yet they are also significantly different. First of all, their gender difference plays a big role. As a girl, Mila wasn't able to work right away. I feel like it was definitely easier for Vargas to find a job in high school. In his essay, he writes, "While in high school, I worked part time at Subway, then at the front desk of the local Y.M.C.A., then at a tennis club, until I landed an unpaid internship at *The Mountain View Voice*, my hometown newspaper." Not only was he able to find a job and make money, he ended up with a job he liked. Mila, on the other hand, works at a restaurant and makes minimum wage. Her boss is not even always on top of her pay checks, and sometimes she has to remind him that he needs to pay her.

Vargas's and Mila's relationships with their families also make their situations different. The fact that Vargas is gay has a complicated effect on his situation. For example, coming out was a relief in a way. In the article, he states, "Coming out about being gay seemed less daunting than coming out about my legal status." It was undoubtedly soothing to have one less secret to worry about. On the other hand, he had to deal with his difficult family. Lolo, his grandfather, was a strict Catholic and being homosexual was not okay in his views. Vargas was kicked out of the house for a few weeks when Lolo found out, but eventually they reconciled. Lolo also brought up the problem that Vargas could not get a green card by marrying an American woman now. This could have been an easy way for him to obtain a citizenship and become a legal immigrant.

Because of her gender and culture, Mila had a lot more restrictions in her life than Vargas did. For instance, I believe that Mila's family is more strict than his. Her family is originally Albanian. Even though they are not extremely religious, the Albanian culture plays a huge role in their lives. Her family didn't allow her to wear certain things and go out at certain times. She also felt the obligation to work and give money to her family, which could be tied back to her sense of responsibility or could be a culturally accepted concept in her homeland.

In school, both Mila and Vargas exceeded expectations and worked very hard for the slightest chance possible. Even though Mila was not involved at all with school activities, she worked 43 hours a week. The fact that she still managed to do her school work and maintain a 4.2 GPA while working is incredible. On the other hand, Vargas focused more on school involvement. He was a known figure in the school and even his principal was aware of his involvement. His principal, Pat Hyland, stated, "'You're at school just as much as I am'" (qtd. in Vargas). This put him one step ahead of the game and was the main reason he was able to get scholarships and attend a good university. Hyland helped find a way for Vargas to attend a university, but Mila knew very few people at school. This put her a step behind in the college process. She attended class, did her homework, and that was it. Teachers loved her for her sense of responsibility and intelligence, but because they didn't know the whole story they were unable to help. Mila was able to save money but simply wasn't given the same opportunities Vargas was given.

Mila revealed her secret to me and few other people, yet Vargas published an essay about his life as an undocumented immigrant. His life definitely took a huge turn telling everyone about his life-long secret. Even though Vargas and Mila are from two different generations, their struggles were and are clearly very similar. Vargas's problem was dramatically brought to the attention of everyone, yet nothing truly happened. When Vargas's essay was first published, he was not deported or arrested; he was simply ignored, and his rights were still stripped away from him. This issue is still prevalent, yet little is done to help find a solution to it. Instead of concentrating on what people like Vargas and Mila can offer with their intelligence and mindset, we limit their resources and chances for success. Deporting someone like Vargas, who knows no other homeland than the U.S and who grew up as an American, is intolerable.

This essay is not about who struggled more. Both Vargas and Mila struggled to live and have basic rights. If anything, I wish Mila would have gotten the chance to read Vargas's essay and learn more about the journey of others like her. Mila and Vargas are part of the "11 million undocumented immigrants in the United States" (Vargas). They are part of 11 million people who have no rights whatsoever living in the U.S.A. I hope that through reading this essay, people can look at this problem differently. Most of us are unaware of what's going on regarding undocumented immigrants, but people like Vargas who decide to stand up and tell the world about their story can truly make a difference. My view changed entirely after I met Mila, and I hope everyone gets the chance to experience what I experienced. We don't choose where we are born or to whom we are born. It makes no sense to me how someone like Vargas, who was raised in the U.S from an early age and who considers himself an American, is not considered one because he is not a legal immigrant. If this is the land of opportunities, then shouldn't everyone, documented or undocumented, be given the same opportunities?

Work Cited

Vargas, Jose. "My Life as an Undocumented Immigrant." *New York Times.* New York Times, 22 June 2011. Web. 2 Nov. 2014.

The Role of Culture

KUDZAI CHIDARIKIRE

What is the relationship between culture and identity? Chidarikire uses essays by Richard Rodriguez and Geeta Kothari to wrestle with this question. Chidarikire's argument grows layer by layer, first drawing on Rodriguez to show that appearance is not a reliable measure of identity, then engaging with Kothari to show how complicated individuals' relationships with culture—or cultures—can be.

Culture is a term that people use to label people of different ethnicities and walks of life. However, people tend to rely on culture too much to define the identity of an individual. People gain certain expectations of an individual based on aspects such as where they are from and how they speak. However, it is incorrect to define someone's identity based solely on their culture because it is but a small part of their entire identity.

In the article "The North American," Richard Rodriguez discusses the concept of race and how it is applied to the different ethnicities in the United States. He claims that race is not a "white and black" concept that should be used to label and identify people (67). Race and ethnicity are not just skin deep; there are many more variables that should be considered before one can determine the identity of another. This idea is seen when Rodriguez states, "For a country that traditionally has taken its understanding of community from blood and color, to have so large a group of Americans identifying themselves by virtue of language or fashion or cuisine or literature is an extraordinary change, and a revolutionary one" (68). Labeling people by the color of their skin is certain to lead to the mislabeling of one's cultural and ethnic identity. Moreover, it is neither a credible nor accurate means of identifying people. For instance, the author says, "You see white Hispanics, black Hispanics, you see brown Hispanics" (68). As you can see from this quote, the color of one's skin is just a part of their outward appearance. It is not a reliable indication of one's culture because even if you are affiliated with a particular culture, you yourself may not meet the typical appearance or behavior that is associated with that culture. Because culture is an intrinsic quality, one cannot conclude what another's culture is by how they look or speak. Rather, people should account for all aspects of culture such as language, cuisine, and traditions to get the most accurate identification. While looking at the color of another's skin provides the quickest hint about their identity, it is often the most vague. In order to get the most informative information of one's identity, one needs to be willing to commit actual time to knowing the individual.

However, identifying someone by their language, cuisine and traditions is not always "full proof." In the article "If You Are What You Eat, Then What Am I?" Geeta Kothari struggles to negotiate the borders that are created from her desire to be a part of both American and Indian cultures. Even though she eats the food of both cultures, she is unable to fully identify as either one. This idea is illustrated when Kothari says, "Now I worry this antipathy toward dal signals something deeper, that somehow I am not my parents' daughter, not Indian, and because I cannot bear the touch and smell of raw meat, though I can eat it cooked (charred, dry, and overdone), I am not American either" (92). Even though Kothari meets the criteria for someone who would be identified as Indian, she still cannot fully identify as Indian because she feels antipathy to the food that she is supposed to love—according to Indian stereotypes. Moreover, she cannot fully identify as American because even though she is able to eat the meat, she cannot bear the touch or scent of it. As a result, these conflicting cultures cause an internal struggle within herself. In this struggle over her cultural identity, Kothari's identity wanders along the borders of these two cultures. Kothari's lack of identity is a result of her belief that her culture defines her. Kothari is convinced that her culture is her identity. Because Kothari holds this belief, she is unable to define who she is when her identity does not blend in with her culture. For that reason, Kothari believes that *she* does not blend in with her culture. However, it's really that her culture does not blend in with her identity. Therefore, Kothari should not let her culture have a major influence on who she is as an individual. Culture is simply a representation of where one comes from, not who one currently is.

The very idea of identity is a complicated matter in itself; some people spend their entire lives trying to discover who they are. This concept is further complicated when the concept of culture is introduced. From birth, one's culture is rooted at the foundation of one's character. For those who are brought up in a background specific to one culture, such as one's homeland, culture plays an enormous role in their daily lives. In these types of backgrounds, the decisions one makes and how one acts are all influenced by culture. People are held to certain standards that are dictated by traditions and values that go several generations back in history. Ultimately, these types of environments mold the identities of their people. If Kothari was raised in India for the majority of her life, she would not have faced the identity struggles she now faces because she would have assumed her culture is her identity. However, Kothari was also raised in America and was exposed to both American and Indian culture. Rather than trying to combine these two cultures and become Indian American, she tries to decide between being Indian and being American. The problem with this choice is that she does not fit into either of these cultures completely. This leads her to believe she lacks an identity because she is unable to meet the criteria for either of the two cultures. However, it's not that she lacks identity; it is because her identity is unique to herself and cannot be classified by either of the two cultures. Therefore, the influence culture has on one's identity is primarily through one's background, although the magnitude of influence it has on one's identity is always up to the individual.

It really is true what they say: "You can't judge a book by its cover," especially if that book is called "Identity." If one's identity were to be represented by a book, culture would take up no more than two or three chapters of it. As people go throughout lives their identity changes, hence the person one was ten years ago is drastically different from who one is at present. One's identity is never fixed for extended lengths of time. The choices and experiences that one goes through on a daily basis each play a role in molding one's identity. Throughout life people are continually editing information in and out of this book called "Identity." Therefore, one will never truly know who they are until the final moments of their life.

Works Cited

Kothari, Geeta. "If You Are What You Eat, Then What Am I?" Vinyard et al 88–92.

Rodriguez, Richard. "The North American." Vinyard et al 66–76.

Vinyard, Deirdre, et al, eds. *Reading and Writing on the Edge*. Boston: Pearson, 2014. Print. Mercury Reader Ser.

Roots

DOREEN FRIMPONG-BRAGO

Frimpong-Brago's essay, which engages questions of identity, language, and assimilation, illustrates how personal experience and sources can be combined to explore complex questions. Her essay also demonstrates how selective, purposeful use of detail and anecdote can engage readers.

The day I set foot in this country, I wondered to myself: Am I going to become a full-blooded American? Will my strong Ghanaian accent make me different from other people or will I learn to slur like everybody else? Will migrating to a new country erase every trace of my culture? To me, my native language was something I held really close to my heart because without it, there was absolutely no other way I could communicate with my family and friends. If there was something I needed to say desperately, that was the best way I could express myself for not every word in my language can be directly translated into English. In an attempt to find answers to some of these questions that were on my mind, I chanced upon a quote from Avnee, a 22-year-old British- and Indian-American, which really hit home: "'I think that where you are at the present is the most important, but at the same time it's essential to not let go of where you've been. You should not have to let go of your roots to be a part of American society'" (qtd. in Maucci). It was when I tried to make sense of this statement that it occurred to me why this quote drew my attention. My grandmother's advice for me before I left for America two years ago was "*Mɛmma wo werɛ mfi baabia wo firi*," which in English means, "Never forget where you come from." It is very important to focus on where you find yourself in the present moment, be it a different country or town, because what you make of it can make or break your future. However, while appreciating and embracing the new ways of life that a new environment has to offer you, you should also keep your cultural traits because they formed the foundation of who you are as an individual now. See them as the seed which was planted in the ground and your new environment as the water that makes the roots of the tree firm and strong.

It seems like a great struggle sometimes for most people to balance their "old life" and their "new life." Most often than not I find myself saying sentences containing a combination of my native language and English. When I want to do my homework while eating, I tell my mum, "Table *no wa dodo, madidi wɔ akonwa no mu na mayɛ me* homework" because the dining table is too tall for me. Surprisingly, at a public gathering or in a public transport like a bus, when I do not want anyone to comprehend whatever important conversation I am having with a family member, I resort to my native language. It might be because I find solace in the fact that I am the only one on the bus who understands what is going on in the conversation or because I want to avoid the eyes that might stare at me when I say what I want to say in English. Usually when immigrants from across different cultures move into the country, it is difficult for them to adapt to new situations, especially a new way of life. Being immersed in a totally foreign culture creates uneasy frictions when they try to fit in, and this was a struggle for one Argentinian- and Peruvian-American, Quetzal Maucci. In her article "Children of Immigrants," she says, "For much of my childhood I felt tension between the culture I was immersed in at school and the culture that my mothers kept alive within our home, the one I returned to each night." Throughout her childhood, Quetzal tells us that all she ate was her mothers' home cooked food, which included meals such as "milanesas and lomo saltado," while her friends at school had peanut butter and jelly for lunch. Even when they were super-excited about Thanksgiving, she said she did not have reason to be because it was not a holiday she celebrated. It is typical of immigrants to try to hold steady to their values and traditions when they find themselves in another culture. However, as time goes on they gradually find a solid ground that satisfies both worlds, balancing their cultural traits with the "new lifestyle" they find themselves in.

In other situations, people feel an imbalance when they are faced with so many stereotypical judgments and discriminations based on how they look and where they are from. They find themselves stuck between a rock and a hard place when they try to defend their place as Americans. Alex Santana, a 21-year-old Spanish- and Dominican-American, says, " 'When others ask, 'Where are you from?' I tend to respond with 'New Jersey.' Usually, they are never satisfied with that answer because for them, it does not explain why I have the last name I have, why my hair is so conspicuously curly, why my skin is brown, and why I am able to speak Spanish' " (qtd. in Maucci). I feel like people always have this painted picture in their minds about how one is supposed to behave and look like because they are from a particular place. Is it good or bad for people to imagine you to be a certain way because you belong to a particular culture? Sometimes I feel like it's actually a good thing because it might portray that you are a true representative of your culture. But it gets bad when other people accuse you wrongly based on that. It reminds me of when people say, "This guy is really smart with science and computers; he must be an Asian"; or "This black woman looks like the violent type; she must be the one who smacked the little girl in the face—let's arrest her." Come to think of it, at what point do these cultural stereotypes escalate to the point where people want to change their identities just because of the way people treat them? Some people try that, but do they really succeed? It is rather important to change the negative perspectives that others have about your culture and not who you are by being the best you can be. On the surface it may look like you are a new person, but deep down on the inside you still possess those original cultural traits you think may have slowly died out.

As I stand here after two years of being in America, speaking in my native language when I want to, mixing it up with English when I can, and embracing the American culture because I live here, am I going to be able to say 10 years from now that I still have every single detail of my culture in me? That I am not sure about because, as Richard Rodriquez says in "The North American," "Culture is fluid. Culture is smoke in the air. You breathe it. You eat it. You notice culture or you don't" (74). Culture diffuses through us and affects us in ways we may not notice. You do not know what you might learn from being in a whole new culture and what it might undo in you after being in contact with it for a period of time. But what I certainly know for sure is I would never forget my roots and where I come from, although I might not acknowledge them in my daily life.

Works Cited

Maucci, Quetzal. "Children of Immigrants." *New York Times*. New York Times, 21 Sept. 2014. Web. 2 Nov. 2014.

Rodriguez, Richard. "The North American." *Reading and Writing on the Edge*. Eds. Deirdre Vinyard et al. Boston: Pearson, 2014. 66–76. Print. Mercury Reader Ser.

The Blending of Cultures in America

MICHAEL MASCIO

*Mascio's use of sources illustrates how multiple texts can be brought into dia-
logue to create a cohesive argument. In particular, he applies Michael Jones-
Correa's ideas about how immigrants become "insiders" in American society
to connect experiences described in Bharati Mukherjee's "Two Ways to Belong
in America" and Quetzal Maucci's "Children of Immigrants."*

When one thinks of culture, they often think of differing traditions and
different ways of life. In the past, it was very easy to distinguish one culture
from another and who fit into each one. But as travel has become ever easier,
immigration has become more and more common. This has led to a blending of many different cultures and has made it more difficult to differentiate
where people fit in to our traditional view of what culture is.

This blending of cultures is especially evident in America, where for various reasons, we have accumulated large populations of people from many
diverse cultures and backgrounds. Most recently, people have come here
voluntarily from all over the world to pursue higher education and employ-
ment opportunities. This is the case with Bharati Mukherjee and her sister
Mira, who initially came to America to study at a university and stayed when
they got jobs (Mukherjee 45). Mira chose to remain culturally Indian, which
influenced the cultural experience of those around her. Bharati, on the other
hand, chose to assimilate and let the culture around her influence her. Based
on appearances, some would say Mira was not a part of American culture
despite living in America because she chose to continue to wear a sari. But an
important part of American culture is its ability to accept other cultures. One
way to be a part of American culture is to be your own culture and let others
be their own culture. That way, you can see what other cultures have to offer
and incorporate them into your own life if you choose.

Michael Jones-Correa, author of "How Immigrants Are Marked as Outsiders," would disagree. He feels there are distinct groups of insiders and
outsiders in America, and immigrants must fulfill three criteria to become

American: a legally defined status, a shared language, and a perception of inclusion. According to his article, immigrants "become insiders when their differences no longer affect the ways they interact with others, the opportunities they have for themselves and their families, and how they participate in politics." Jones-Correa's criteria of an outsider create a divide between who is American and who is not. Despite his seemingly black-and-white picture of what it means to belong to American culture, he acknowledges that being an insider is not as clear cut as being an outsider. Just because someone fulfills his checklist, that doesn't automatically make them American. The third item on his list, a perception of inclusion, can be the hardest to obtain because it relies both on the immigrants' feelings about others and on others' feelings towards them, which they have no control over. But this is an important point that is often overlooked. To belong to a culture, one has to feel that they are accepted by that culture (i.e., the people who already make up that culture). The need to be accepted by the people in a certain culture may lead one to adopt more of its customs and forfeit more of one's own. This generally only applies to people who are moving from one culture to another. When you are born into a culture and your parents are already a part of that culture, they make sure you have that sense of belonging.

This is an important aspect that children of immigrants can feel is especially difficult to overcome. New immigrants often feel connected to their original country, even if they obtain insider status as laid out by Jones-Correa. Inevitably, they will retain much of their culture simply because it is what they have always known. This contributes to the blending of cultures that we see especially in America. Their children, on the other hand, who experience culture both from their family and from their peers, may feel torn by these two competing cultures. Quetzal Maucci, who is the daughter of immigrants from Peru and Argentina, says she "felt tension between the culture I was immersed in at school and the culture that my mothers kept alive within our home." In her photo essay "Children of Immigrants" in the *New York Times*, Maucci tells of her life as the second generation of her family to live in America and compiles quotes from others in the same situation about how they deal with their cultural experience. Many of the people quoted express the same sentiment: they do not feel fully integrated into either their parents' culture or American culture. They instead feel stuck in between, not fully belonging to one or the other. This is likely influenced greatly by how well their parents have integrated with American culture. Someone like Bharati, who fully integrated with American culture and fulfilled completely Jones-Correa's criteria for inclusion, would probably have children who struggle very little with their cultural identity. Mira's children, on the other hand, would almost certainly feel stuck between two worlds because she refused to give up her Indian heritage.

Both immigrants and their children struggle with culture but in very different ways. An immigrant can choose what aspects of each culture they want to incorporate into their life. It is also somewhat easier for them because they have made the decision to move to a new country. They have an idea of what to expect, even if they don't know exactly what their lives will be like. Their children, on the other hand, are thrust into a situation they know very little about. Even immigrants who choose to completely adopt a new culture will likely wish to retain some traditions. As a result, their children have to choose aspects of their culture before they even know what the different traditions and customs really mean. They further contribute to the blending of cultures, and as they grow up, they share their cultural experience with other people. They further blend cultures until we end up with what we see today: a mix of cultures from all over the world.

Works Cited

Jones-Correa, Michael. "How Immigrants Are Marked as Outsiders." *New York Times*. New York Times, 18 Nov. 2012. Web. 2 Nov. 2014.

Maucci, Quetzal. "Children of Immigrants." *New York Times*. New York Times, 21 Sept. 2014. Web. 2 Nov. 2014.

Mukherjee, Bharati. "Two Ways to Belong in America." *Reading and Writing on the Edge*. Eds. Deirdre Vinyard et al. Boston: Pearson, 2014. 44–48. Print. Mercury Reader Ser.

The Ethos of Anzaldúa's "How to Tame a Wild Tongue"

JENNIFER OCHAETA

In this rhetorical analysis, Ochaeta uses the concepts of ethos and pathos to analyze the effectiveness of Gloria Anzaldúa's essay, "How to Tame a Wild Tongue." Ethos and pathos are two ways writers can persuade or influence readers. When using pathos, writers appeal to readers' emotions; when using ethos, writers use their own identity or position to influence readers' responses. By analyzing her own experiences as a reader, Ochaeta develops a nuanced argument explaining how Anzaldúa's essay impacts different audiences.

The world we live in today can be considered a prejudiced one, where some feel the need to place themselves at the top of a hierarchy. In "How to Tame a Wild Tongue," author Gloria Anzaldúa discusses what it was like growing up in southwest Texas on the border of Mexico. In southwest Texas her language can be considered inferior to the regular English language people speak. Anzaldúa talks about her languages and how her languages are a part of who she is as a Mexican-American woman. She speaks of the identity of a Chicano and the struggle Chicanos go through to try to be something else. The author believes that the struggles Chicanos go through can be solved by everyone putting in as much of an effort as the Chicanos do to understand others. Anzaldúa discusses how her different forms of English and Spanish are a part of who she and her people are, and that they should not have to be silenced or changed. Throughout the essay her voice really shines through, and her passion about this is revealed. Though her point comes across, the main question is whether or not her message becomes less effective to some readers by the overwhelming emotions she portrays.

Anzaldúa begins her essay with an easily relatable metaphor: "'We're going to have to control your tongue,' the dentist says pulling out all the metal. … My [Anzaldúa's] mouth is a motherlode. … My tongue keeps pushing out the wads of cotton, pushing back drills, the long thin needles. 'I've never seen anything as strong or as stubborn,' he says. And I think, how do you tame a wild tongue, train it to be quiet?" (Anzaldúa 156). The idea of using such a literal metaphor is so that the reader can picture a person at the dentist and the actual physical sensation of him shoving things into their mouth to suppress their tongue. This makes it easy for the reader at this point to comprehend the emotions of frustration the author portrays and to begin to sympathize. Most readers can get an idea of what the essay will be about through the metaphor, but Anzaldúa still makes a separate point through this metaphor that only one certain type of audience can understand: the Spanish speakers.

When reading the essay, Spanish speakers can find it easier to pick up the main message of the essay through the metaphor. Her Spanish speaking audience can make the connection between the word "tongue" and its Spanish translation, *lengua*. The word *lengua* also means language, foreshadowing for her Spanish speaking audience that she isn't just referring to the actual tongue but overall to her language. As her essay carries on, her tone and stories continue to target different audiences in different ways. This is where the pathos of the audience begins to differentiate, depending on which audience she is specifically targeting.

To play to her women audience, Anzaldúa brings up a common proverb: "*En boca cerrada no entran moscas*" (Anzaldúa 157). She then translates this to "Flies don't enter a closed mouth" (81). When going over this phrase, she mentions how women in her culture are silenced more often than men, and she brings up the fact that only the feminine form is used in this Spanish phrase and any other involving silencing. She brings this up for her readers, especially women, to understand the irritation she felt growing up. Even though it is clear that she is mainly aiming toward women, any type of reader can still read the proverbs and understand the ethos she is trying to portray. As her essay continues, her tone changes and she starts to illustrate her message by changing her ethos.

At first, the Spanish phrases are a way to connect with her audience. As the essay progresses, she no longer seems to be trying to get some of the readers to sympathize but instead empathize. By increasing the Spanish sayings to more than half of her essay, she allows the non-Spanish speaking readers to start to feel as frustrated as she once felt. For example, when discussing the struggles of identity in not only her life but in the lives of other Chicanos, a huge point in her essay, she writes, "*Tenemos que hacer la lucha. Quién está protegiendo los ranchos de mi gente? Quién está tratando de cerrar la fisura entre la india y el blanco en nuestra sangre? El chicano, sí, el chicano que andan como un ladrón en su propia casa*" (Anzaldúa 167). Anzaldúa purposely gives no translation to this paragraph. In it she is saying how the Chicanos have to work hard to blend in with others. They themselves have to work hard to be at one with Americans though they themselves are a type of American, showing how they work harder than typical Americans. Though it may seem strange, the author is getting her point across to one audience by almost angering them and really getting them to understand what it felt like to her growing up. However, to her Spanish-speaking audience she is giving this beautiful motivation to work hard and try to let their identity show. She uses the "we" form of the verbs to really express her passion of Latino-Americans and how they should express their culture. Anzaldúa is empowering them. She is motivating them to see her point and firing her passion inside of them, giving them a sense of unity.

Anzaldúa's essay speaks out to me as a Spanish speaker. I could feel all the emotions she was portraying to each audience. As I was growing up, I saw my school and town change from a mainly white community to an extremely diverse one. I started off in a class with only five Latino kids total and ended with almost half of my graduating class being Latino. Through that, I could understand all the emotions each kind of reader can feel. I can see how and why people would get frustrated not being able to understand because that is how most of my friends felt as our community became more diverse. I could also feel her empowering words go through me as I read the Spanish phrases. Overall I believe Anzaldúa's ethos, though it may seem overpowering, is truly effective for her pathos. I believe that each reader will feel exactly what she wants that specific type of reader to feel. In the end, her essay brings across the point that each person needs to put in the full effort to really understand one another and not allow one another to feel inferior.

Work Cited

Anzaldúa, Gloria. "How to Tame a Wild Tongue." *Reading and Writing on the Edge*. Eds. Deirdre Vinyard et al. Boston: Pearson, 2014. 156–67. Print. Mercury Reader Ser.

Tongue and Language

JIAQI WEI

Combining elements of summary and response as well as rhetorical analysis, Wei explores how different readers—including herself—might respond to Amy Tan's "Mother Tongue." As Wei points out, learning "normal English" is a process that takes many years; mastering academic English can take even longer. By addressing the reader directly, Wei argues for accepting language difference and valuing immigrants' experiences.

In the whole world, there are tens of thousands of languages and tongues. In normal life, we may mix different kinds of language together to communicate with others in order to make others understand our meaning. Actually, there is a kind of special tongue or language in the world, and we can call it "mother tongue." Literally, "mother tongue" means the style of pronunciation from Amy Tan's mother described in the essay "Mother Tongue." Through telling the stories of her mother who as a classic immigrant just can speak broken English in America, Tan exposes some real barriers that immigrants normally face. This story makes me feel a kind of familiar feeling. As an international student who studies in America, I experience a lot of similar events.

In "Mother Tongue," Tan talks about some stories about her mother's language, which is a kind of broken language. Tan is an Asian American writer. She has a Chinese mother. Many years ago, her mother immigrated into California from Shanghai, China. Obviously, it may be a little bit difficult for her to speak authentic English. In that period of time, her mother might not have enough basis of English. In addition, English is also a difficult language to learn, as I know from my own experiences. Fortunately, for me, I really understand her mother's situation because as an international student who also comes from China, I have had similar experiences. English is a kind of second language for me and when I use it to communicate with others, it also sometimes makes me feel uncomfortable. But using the broken English is also a normal and high frequency thing for me. Therefore, it is not difficult to understand the situation that the author's mother has.

Tan talks about the two different kinds of English in "Mother Tongue." The first one is the normal English, which she uses in her daily life, and another one is a kind of broken English, which is used by her mother to communicate with her. In fact, her mother is not good at English, but Tan clearly understands what her mother says. There are some interesting examples about her mother asking Tan to call other people for her. As Tan mentions in the article, "When I was fifteen, she used to have me call people on the phone to pretend I was she. In this guise, I was forced to ask for information or even to complain and yell at people who had been rude to her. One time it was a call to her stockbroker in New York" (133). The problem the author is facing is similar for many immigrant families. Some immigrants do not have extremely good basis of English, even though they may live in America for many years and can communicate with others and understand others' language. In addition, the broken English always bring a lot of problems for the part of immigrants. They constantly are ridiculed by other people or deceived by others. We cannot deny that author's experience can cause resonance in immigrant groups.

For you, you may not really understand Amy Tan's experience because maybe in your home all of your family members speak the normal English and you do not have a Chinese mother. However, personally, I have lots of similar experiences because I have a Chinese mother. In addition, I also have a Chinese grandmother.

As you know, in China we have different traditional languages in different regions. My grandmother is not good at Mandarin. In my hometown, people frequently speak a kind of traditional language, which is Ningbo Hua, so when she communicates with other people, she often mixes two kinds of language together. My grandmother's communicating style does not cause any problem when she communicates with our family members or chats with people who live in our city, which makes me think that is the reason why it is not difficult for her to convey her opinions to me. Several sentences in "Mother Tongue" give some idea of this: "[O]ver the twenty years we've been together I've often used that same kind of English with [my husband], and sometimes he even uses it with me. It has become our language of intimacy, a different sort of English that relates to family talk, the language I grew up with" (131). There is a similar situation in our family. My grandmother's mixed language already becomes a normal or official language in our family because in past years, all of my family members usually use this kind of mixed language to communicate with her. However, when she goes outside to travel and goes shopping, she faces some awkward situations, such as when others cannot understand her language clearly. Other people who do not understand Ningbo Hua may feel confused about my grandmother's language, so she frequently is fooled by others. She also is a teacher and taught in a middle school. In recent years, more and more children whose parents work in our city study in the school of our city. When my grandmother applies her mixed language to talk about the contents of books, they cannot always understand clearly her language and even make fun of her language after class. My grandmother constantly feels really helpless.

For you, maybe there is not any immigrant experience in your family or you do not have any friends who are immigrants. When you touch "Mother Tongue," you might not have similar feeling as I have.

In "Mother Tongue," Tan mentions, "I have been thinking about all this lately, about my mother's English, about achievement tests. Because lately I've been asked, as a writer, why there are not more Asian Americans represented in American literature. Why are there few Asian Americans enrolled in creative writing programs? Why do so many Chinese students go into engineering?" (135). Obviously, it is a sociological question. I think there are some social prejudices. Maybe in most people's opinion, American people can do better at literature. Maybe we just are limited by this kind of traditional idea, which is Asian people should do better than American people in subjects like math, physics, and so on. Asian parents may think their children cannot do well in literature and try to make their children develop in science subjects. Therefore, when Asian American children are young, they are forced to learn a lot of things about math and not literature or writing. In my opinion, sometimes Asian American also can do better in literature and writing articles than the American people whose families have been in the United States for many generations. We just get wrong indoctrination or incorrect idea from our elders or parents. Actually, Amy Tan is a good and obvious example for us. She is a quite successful author even though she also is an Asian American.

In reality, social prejudices may be a large social problem. We usually can see some people are ignored because they speak terrible or unskilled language. For example, when some foreign people speak terrible English to order a meal in American restaurant, the waiters always feel impatient, which is similar to an example which Tan talks about in "Mother Tongue." When her mother uses her broken English to communicate, she gets unfair treatment; however, when Tan uses perfect English, the attitude of the doctor becomes better (133–134). Therefore, the social prejudices of language exist, and we need to try our best to remove them.

Anyway, immigrants are a special group of people in the world. We can find the mixed background from them, which is specific and also is wonderful. We need to respect them, remove the prejudice, and also learn a lot of things from them. Now, immigrants are a small group of people. However, the population mobility still increases in recent years. Maybe in the future, immigration will become mainstream, and you and I also will become a part of it. So will you change your attitude to this part of mainstream population?

Work Cited

Tan, Amy. "Mother Tongue." *Reading and Writing on the Edge*. Eds. Deirdre Vinyard et al. Boston: Pearson, 2014. 130–6. Print. Mercury Reader Ser.

Part 2

Essays from
College Writing

Inquiring into Self

Preface

College Writing begins by asking students to examine the "self"—or one of our many selves—as a text in a unit called "Inquiring into Self." The self, after all, is a text that absolutely must be read and re-read with great attentiveness, for it shapes how we understand, interpret, and interact with the world. Using the writing process (generative writing and reading, composing and revising, giving and receiving feedback to and from fellow writers, and editing), students are asked to discover new insights about how their contexts have shaped them. The challenge is to read their stories and bodies as histories and to begin to re-see themselves through the lenses of social contexts—e.g., towns, churches, athletic teams, ethnic communities, and more. Here, students write meaningfully about their own lives. The following essays illustrate this inquiry into self and invite a close audience of classmates to engage with each writer's experiences and critical reflections.

Wrestling with God

RUTHNEY BENJAMIN

Ruthney Benjamin is engaged in a powerful spiritual and emotional struggle. How can she remain true to her sexual identity while maintaining a relationship with her parents and her church, who view her lifestyle as "an abomination"? The essay's structure, diction, tone, and her appeals to logos and pathos all contribute to Benjamin's representation of this struggle.

"We want our daughter back."

"Well Dad, it's not like I went anywhere to begin with." The thought briefly darts across my mind, but I shut it down quickly and reluctantly nod my head in agreement with every piercing sentence that spits out of my parents' mouths. How could I not? After all, my parents are wise adults; therefore they are always right, aren't they? So with my eyes burning a hole through the wooden floor in my parent's bedroom, I continuously mutter muffled agreements and fight back the tears that flood my heavy eye sockets.

Of course I wasn't a lesbian. I was still attracted to boys. The Devil just had a firm grasp on my life, and I was letting him and his demons take me down the evil lesbian path. I was so deep in a pit of no return that I had already been in numerous relationships with girls, and even expressed the forbidden emotion of love, making plans for the future with one of them. To my parents, I had become a void soul, lost in this massive planet drenched in sin; it was like I had become a spindly skeleton who had long embraced death. What they wanted was the little Ruthney they had become attached to in my adolescence, but they were naive to the fact that my innocence wouldn't last forever. They disregarded the fact that I didn't grow up to be who they had prayed for me to be, and they disregarded the fact that I broke away from their grasp and became my own person. And thus I was the prodigal daughter they begged on their knees to come back, to return to being the make-believe shadow of a daughter they had pleaded for so badly. They didn't realize, however, that I hadn't gone anywhere—I was just sprouting into who I always was.

"This is not who Christ made you to be."

Thank you, Pastor, for never failing to remind me of my wrongdoings and my status as an abomination to the Seventh-Day Adventist Church. I can't blame my parents and my pastor for their extremism, for it is the Adventist belief that homosexuality originates from the Devil, and all who partake in it are doomed to eternal hellfire unless saved and redeemed by the Lord Jesus Christ. Some may view it as a wee bit extreme, but beliefs are beliefs. In fact, I chewed and swallowed everything I was told because I, too, was an active member of the Seventh-Day Adventist Church, born and raised. I knew that gay wasn't okay (according to the Church), that gay people go to hell, that they would be excluded from the Church, and so on and so forth. I had no other choice but to confess my sin and engage in what seemed like decade-long Bible studies and prayer sessions in the Pastor's stuffy cramped office—the very last place I wanted to be. It became sickening to have to sit there and force myself to listen to his tirade about who Christ wants me to be, all as I twiddled my thumbs and felt guilty for actions that seemed perfectly okay to me.

"Jesus died on the Cross so you could be saved, not for you to become a lesbian."

I wish I could say it was easy for me to accept these beliefs that I had grown up with and continue living my Christ-fearing life. As much as I wanted to pick up all three of my worn and torn Bibles and testify to my wonderful merciful Savior and praise Him for how He pulled me from the deep bottomless pit that I was digging for myself, I couldn't bring myself to do so. There was always that miniscule voice in the back of my thoughts urging me to revolt! Revolt against my beliefs because who was I fooling—of course I didn't agree with most of the crap I was being spoon-fed. I'm a human being, not a robot, and therefore instructions and meaningless information cannot be simply placed into my system, forcing me to follow whatever I was being commanded to follow. I faithfully attended church every Sabbath morning, but I increasingly struggled with being able to wrap my mind around the religion's concepts. How could it be so easy to spread love and preach acceptance for all while totally excluding particular groups of people for their personal preferences? This had me grappling with whether Adventism, or even Christianity, was worth believing in, and I nonchalantly began to distance myself away from my home church and all the members in it. Who was God to tell me who I could and could not become? Why did my beliefs have to be set in stone, preventing me from having convictions of my own?

"If you go on like this, you will live a miserable life."

So began my internal battle of beliefs that succeeded in consuming my every-day life. I longed to be devoted to Christ and walk with Him on the spiritual journey that I had always desired, but it was made clear by the religious voices surrounding me that it would be 100 percent impossible if I continued on the "demonic" path that was destroying me. So I would lie on my bed for countless nights, arguing with God, salty streams running down the sides of my cheeks, debating whether I wanted to live a hopeless lie or dwell in excommunicated freedom. Why couldn't I just be able to express myself however I wanted with-out being bombarded with bricks from people who supposedly love me? My parents never stopped talking about the miserable life I was going to live if I kept up my girl-loving actions, but to me, my misery had begun long before my life even began.

"We want you to be normal."

It's crazy to think that thousands, maybe even millions of teenage Christians go through the same heart-wrenching process as I did—every single day, dawn to dusk. Some probably even have it worse, contemplating if their precious lives are worth living, with a Bible in one hand and a pistol in the other. They struggle to identify who they are as individuals because they are forcibly torn into two halves: the Christian half and the gay half. Outside influences are forever steering them into a single direction, though both would suit them just fine. What some branches of the Christian Church fail to realize is that we teenagers do not want or plead for a struggle that messes up our lives. If it were a simple choice to make, wouldn't we take the road frequently traveled and find the easy route out of the dilemma? We wrestle with God, wrack-ing our brains, ripping the hairs out of our heads, striving to be what is so dogmatically defined as *normal*! We are mentally split into a million pieces because our clergy members, our parents, our society advocates for us to be unique, to be original, to be *ourselves*, but we can never really do that without being admonished, squashed, or tuned out.

"You will never be happy."

I love my family, I would die defending my religion, and I love Jesus Christ, my Lord and Savior. I know for a fact that this love is not unrequited, so I and the thousands of others who are in the same position that I was once in should never have to undergo the atrocities that I underwent. When I got baptized at the age of thirteen, I'll admit I was young and on the clueless side, but I definitely know that I did not sign up for a lifetime of self-hatred, sui-cidal thoughts, public shaming, familial disowning, etc. I got baptized because

God's love is both unfailing and unconditional, and I knew that no matter who I was, what I did, or what my status was, He would never cease to love me. I don't believe that I'll never be happy, and I don't believe that I'm going to die because I take interest in relationships outside heterosexual ones. I do believe, however, that I am "fearfully and wonderfully made and marvelous are [the Lord's] works." Happiness is a state of mind that cannot be taken away from us and one that I, in particular, refuse to give away. I can be happy whether or not others believe I won't be because I have my own God-given state of mind that can't be interfered with or stripped away.

"You will die."

Thank you for me reminding me, Mom and Dad, but it's already clear to me how the cycle of life works. Just like death, human nature is not something controlled. I want to tell my parents that I'm the same Ruthney they've raised and witnessed grow throughout eighteen years. I want to tell my parents that regardless of the gender of the person I decide to lie next to at night, I will live a full, exciting, and happy life. I want to tell my parents that I haven't given up on God, and I will never give up on them either, even though they've given up on me. It's easy to fake it to my parents, to my church, to society that I've transformed into who they wanted me to be, although I don't know how long I'll be forced to have to fake it. What I do know is that no outside influence has the right to command who I have to be or what set of rules and regulations I have to conform to. God created me as an individual capable of making my own decisions and walking the path that I set out for myself, not the one that is set up for me. I know that once God is with me, no one can stand against me, and as long as my hand is in His, He will love me no matter who I am.

A Hedge Back Home

SAM HOLZMAN

Sam Holzman begins his essay with a song lyric that becomes a metaphor for the conflict he feels about his affluent hometown that is filled with "monotonous, identical mansions with their white picket fences." Summer vacations with his cousins in rural Virginia have opened his eyes to another view of the world— and exploring other worlds is what he believes he must do to define his identity and discover a place to call home, "where [he] can see straight and clear over whatever hedge it may hold." He develops his essay with vibrant sensory descrip- tion and poetic devices that invite the reader into his experience.

"We had a hedge back home in the suburbs over which I never could see."

—The Clash

There is a long, green field in a small town called Sumerduck, Virginia. It sits behind a small house with walls painted a dull gray, the color chipping away from the wood with each passing year. It is as if the home is an afterthought, a shelter for when the sun falls and darkness sweeps over the glistening beauty of the yard. I have only seen this field in the summertime, when the thick sunlight tints the tips of the tall blades of grass white as they sway in the warm breeze. Five small dogs chase each other across the field with the same intensity I have witnessed each of the last ten years I have visited. A black pig runs among them, trying desperately to keep up despite its short legs. On the patio overlooking the field, my three cousins and my older brother sit under the shade of the rooftop, sipping cold beer. They smile and offer my younger brother and me drinks when our parents fall into their sunburnt slumber under their umbrella.

Every summer I spend a few weeks at this small house with the vast yard, and when I return home, I wonder exactly what it is that enchants me about that little town in Virginia. There are few practical ways in which it is superior to my hometown of Avon, Connecticut, where the roads are smooth, the grass is finely trimmed, most of the community is rich, and the houses are enormous. I live on the edge of town in an average-sized house, but if I take a few turns,

I find myself in a neighborhood where each house is four times the size of my cousins' humble Virginia home. Yet even with all the benefits of living in an illustrious place, I would find myself dissatisfied every time I came home. When I stumbled upon my older brother's CD collection (and dusted off each individual one in the bin with a rag so I could read the covers), I found the words to the strange emotion I was feeling.

I was sixteen when I first heard The Clash's "Lost in the Supermarket." The song is built on a clever metaphor: songwriter Joe Strummer uses a supermarket as a microcosm for the world. When one line blasted through my cheap, overused headphones, it was like something ignited in my brain. Something that it had been waiting patiently to do but needed this push: "We had a hedge back home in the suburbs over which I never could see." I remember that warm August night that I sat in bed listening to that album, the way my head perked up like a dog's would after making some interesting discovery. I rewound that one line at least a dozen times. *Could they really mean what I think they do?* If I had heard the song for the first time now that I am older and have been exposed to countless literary devices, I would have recognized the metaphor immediately. At that time, however, in whatever raw and youthful ignorance I still had left, I thought about that line for hours.

There was never a doubt in my mind that music could serve as an outlet for reflection; I could relate to songs from a very young age, but on a purely superficial level. A wild rap song would remind me of nights out with friends. A melodramatic pop-punk song could conjure memories of a silly middle school relationship gone wrong (and it still makes me cringe when I peruse my old iTunes collection). The possibility that a piece of music could so accurately echo an emotion on such a large scale, however, was completely new.

Just like the song goes, I had a hedge I couldn't see over in my nice suburban home. Literal tall bushes or shrubbery didn't surround my house. The hedges I couldn't see over were the monotonous, identical mansions with their white picket fences and smooth driveways. They were the endless line of chain restaurants and the lack of any place completely unique to my town. They were the subtly dismissive ways people would talk to and about each other, as if friendly conversation was only a roadblock on their path to wherever they were headed.

When I parked my car in Nick's driveway on a cool summer night, I could already hear the laughter and the crackling of driftwood landing in the bonfire in the backyard. I may have been smiling as I approached the rest of my friends, but I couldn't help the rumbling in my gut that reminded me it would be the last time we'd all be together for a while. One last summer night before we scattered across the nation to our various universities.

We sat with our bare feet against the logs that surrounded the fire and reminisced on all our lost moments of pride and regret. When the cooler of drinks contained nothing but ice and empty bottles we didn't feel like carrying to the trashcan, we set our eyes on the future.

"Why wouldn't you want to live somewhere like here?" one of my best friends said, gesturing sloppily at all the houses around us. "Get a good job, nice house, we have all we could want in Avon."

Still red from the sunburn I'd come home with from Virginia, I sipped my drink and nodded my head, trying to understand why my friend's words were bothering me. I looked out at the street of my buddy's neighborhood. In the midnight blackness, the dim streetlights only partially cast brightness over the row of large houses, diminishing them of any distinguishable detail and making them appear identical.

I wondered at what point my friend, who shared so much in common with me, and I went separate ways in our thoughts about the future and our homes. Maybe if I never paid any mind to the wide field behind my cousins' house, maybe if I never left my hometown at all, I would be able to reside there in complete contentment and peace until I grew old. I would never be able to see over that hedge because I would never know it was there.

But I did leave home. I did recognize the "hedge back home in the suburbs" that kept me from seeing the rest of the country and the rest of the world, and in a way kept me from figuring out who I was. Only by stepping out from behind the hedge can I truly know myself, and I am still far from any certainty in that regard. What I know is that I am intrigued by unique, vast stretches of land, by roads that that feel different under my tires, by the potential to drive for a day and find myself in a place that seems worlds away from the one I just left. I will always hold a fondness for the place I grew up, for that hedge back home that kept me from filling my head with these big ideas too early on in my youth. Now that I have grown both physically and intellectually, I hope to one day find a place where I can make a new home. A place where I can see straight and clear over whatever hedge it may hold.

Naiveté

JENNIFER MULOMBE

Jennifer Mulombe's essay "Naiveté" reveals her struggle to maintain her identity as her naïve excitement about immigrating to America from Congo, Africa, melts away under the glare of naïve prejudice. Mulombe's vivid, engaging description and precise selection of detail enable her to write with nuance and complexity about exploring her own identity, resolving personal conflict, and recognizing the multiple identities of her "birthplace with the good, the bad, and the in-between."

I was excited. I was beyond excited. I had all these images of America—images from movies I had seen, actors I had loved, and singers I held as my idols. And now, I finally had the chance to see this country. I expected America to be everything I had ever heard of or seen on TV.

My family and I departed on March 5, 2005 from the airport in Kinshasa, Congo, proceeded to Switzerland, and then continued along to America. My older sister scored the window seats both times, and I kept complaining about it until my father sternly shushed me, ordering me to settle down. It was my first time flying, and my stomach was full of knots of excitement and nervousness. We arrived in Boston the next day in the early afternoon. It was undeniably cold. As soon as we stepped outside of Logan, we were met with a gush of bitter wind that instantly numbed my cheeks. I finally had my first glimpse of this unfamiliar country.

There were no palm trees, fruit trees, or even any leafy trees in sight. It was not noisy; there were no street vendors or shrieking cab drivers fighting for customers. I couldn't hear the squawking birds or see the neighborhood children playing a vicious game of tag. There was a slight rustling of the naked tree branches, still not sprouting after a long, brutal winter. It was bright and sunny, yet still terribly freezing. The sidewalks were covered with snow banks—not pearly white like I had envisioned—but snow that had turned into a brown-grayish mush. Quickly grasping my father's hands, I stood in awe and excitement, taking in the cars, the people, and the buildings in a matter of seconds. As a nine year old, I still did not fully grasp the true meaning of what it meant to leave the place you were raised in, to completely uproot your life for a new land with a different culture, different way of conduct, and a very different language. The only thought running through my mind was "Wow!"

We quickly settled in, and I started school a month after we arrived. The administration assigned me an ESL teacher, Mrs. White, to speed my English learning process. Mrs. White had taken French way back in college, so she had forgotten a few things. She was in her mid-fifties, and had a continuous habit of always taking off her glasses, rubbing her eyes, then putting them on once again. Despite her age, the elderly lady always smiled and taught me with energy, patience, and kindness. The school material proved to be very demanding with a brand new language. But Mrs. White and I were a team, and together we fought through the homework, struggled through the writing exercises, and constantly read, starting in French and then moving to English. I worked extremely hard and soon enough, I quickly started to pick up English faster than anyone else in my family.

I went to my first American birthday party in May; everyone in my class was invited. It was Kaitlyn's birthday party, and I did not even want to go. Kaitlyn was the girl who laughed at me when I told her I liked her yellow hair. I did not care for her much after that. She was also the girl who asked me about "my" huts. She looked at me disbelievingly when I patiently explained to her I had never seen a hut in my life. I spoke of my house, enclosed in twenty feet of cement wall with a big central gate. I told her how I missed our avocado, mango, and lemon trees that I attempted to climb—without success—every single day. My room overlooked the backyard; it was big, filled with boxes of toys, memories of dolls, and collections of cars from my tomboy phase. My favorite place in the house was the veranda, with its big comfy couches and the huge stony fireplace that was never used. In a country that was hot all year round, I never really understood why it was there. There was always an overwhelming smell of fresh bread from the *la boulangerie* a couple houses down. Kaitlyn, the yellow-haired girl, did not believe any of this, and instead ran away saying I was lying and that everyone knew Africa only had huts.

There were many things I missed from back home. I missed *La Fikin*, the amusement park fifteen minutes from our house. I missed playing with my friends back home. And I missed my family. It did not take me long to realize that not many people were educated about my country. The questions I received grew even more ridiculous and tremendously shameful. "*Did you sleep with animals?*" "*Don't all diseases come from Africa?*" I started wishing that I could lie about where I was born. "*How come people over there are always dirty?*"

I began to hate the word African. I hated what it implied: that I was born in a country full of problems, a country constantly at war, with a never-ending high rate of poverty. *"My mom and I always send ten dollars to children in need in Africa."* I wanted to scream at the top of my lungs that this was not the country I remembered. *"Wow you are actually smart, being from Africa and all."* It was humiliating and degrading. As soon as I muttered I was African, there were always some judgments, ranging from looks of pity from adults to shameful questions from the adolescents. To people who did not know me, I started to lie, quickly claiming that my family was born there but I was born here. I did not receive any looks or questions then.

In 4th grade, there was a big cultural week, a week where students could display their families' ancestries. You could perform, dance, make and share food, or build a project to help others better understand your culture. In addition, we had a school-wide assembly where we met a Rwandese motivational speaker. She spoke about the Rwandan Genocide, the genocide that killed thousands and thousands of people. It was a horrific event, yet she spoke of her country with a sense of pride. Her eyes gleamed with love of her country despite the fact that it was not perfect. I did not understand that. After the lecture, I approached her to quietly ask her a question that had been burning through my thoughts. "How can you be happy when you have experienced so much hurt, so much loss? How can you love your country when you have lost your family and loved ones because of it?" She gave me one simple answer in Swahili, an answer that took a while for me to understand. *"Mimi ni mimi kwa sababu ya utamaduni wangu." I am me because of my culture.* I did not understand then. As I got older, I started to know why I did things differently from others. It was because of my principles. The way I behaved or handled a situation was all because of how I was raised, and my beliefs played a huge role in my life. I started understanding that quote through the experiences of my life. And that is when I became proud.

Yes, I am African, born and raised. My mother descended from the Mungala Tribe and my father was from the Muswahili and Muluba Tribes. I speak four languages, but I understand five. I am proud of my culture and of my traditions. I still carry on what I had been taught ever since I was a little child. I respect my elders; I take pride in education; and as a girl, I am able to take care of any houses by cleaning and cooking. I am me because of my culture.

I quickly learned as I got older that some of the small-minded people I had met were not at all how everyone was in the U.S. Most people, in fact, are always awed as soon as they learn of my birthplace, Congo, Africa. They quickly exclaim that "they can't hear an accent!" I have long stopped listening to ignorant questions. The media plays a big role in the depiction of the poverty in Africa. I understand that. But what people need to understand is yes, my country has several issues: politically, economically, and socially. It is not as technologically advanced as the U.S., and the government is made up of corrupted officials. Congo is modernized: yes, there are cars, there are planes, computers, and phones. There are schools, apartments, hotels, gyms, and malls. Yes, there are tall buildings and even lights!

I had the chance to be raised in a beautiful home with my beautiful family. I had clothes, shoes, food, and water. I attended a private Catholic school and went to church every Sunday like a good Christian. Life was still not perfect. I have multiple family members who have passed away as a result of wars and rebel attacks. Yet, I am proud of my birthplace with the good, the bad, and the in-between. It will always be my birthplace, and I pray that one day my generation and the generations to come can help put our country on a path of peace and prosperity.

An Attempt to Change the World

JESSICA MURPHY

Inspired by her teacher's lessons on Mahatma Gandhi, Jessica Murphy decides to live according to Gandhi's command to "Be the change you wish to see in the world." Although she participates in many worthy activities that could change both her town and school, Murphy discovers instead that her efforts are foiled by her own limitations, the confines of her context, and the vicissitudes of life. She structures her essay according to the evolution of her quest and her more mature understanding of what Gandhi is really asking of her—and all of us.

Be the change you wish to see in the world.

Gandhi paraphernalia littered the room: posters, some proudly displayed on each wall and others still rolled up, sitting on shelves and waiting to be hung; lithograph pictures of the Salt March and previous students' exceptional work. The quote was stenciled in navy on the wall above my honors world history teacher's desk, accompanied by a portrait of the man who spoke those words. He was bald, which displayed his prominent ears, and his round glasses framed intelligent eyes. Two more tiny Gandhi faces were painted on the support beams—one in hot pink and another in forest green. Needless to say, my pony-tailed, fully bearded, flannel-wearing teacher had a bit of an obsession. His passion for Gandhi was contagious, and we eagerly anticipated our future learning.

Before February vacation, we were told the greatest unit in all of history would be upon us the Monday we returned. We all knew what was in our future: Gandhi. For two weeks (almost quadruple the amount of time recommended in public school guidelines), we learned everything Gandhi. When most of us were still wearing Abercrombie T-shirts created in a sweatshop, Gandhi spun his own thread to make clothes. When most of us couldn't convince our friends to join the yearbook club just for fun, he inspired a nation to peacefully revolt against the British crown.

As a freshman, I couldn't even imagine personally leading a two hundred and forty mile march for twenty-four days. The Salt March received world recognition for the Indian Civil Disobedience Movement. Furthermore, it inspired its own citizens to join the movement to fight against their own injustices.

My inspiration and awe were followed by a tinge of jealousy. Why wasn't there a deep social issue in my sleepy suburban town that I could fix through peaceful protesting? The Natick police weren't going to beat me with their batons for protesting the school lunch choices. How could I change the world if there weren't any problems here?

Nevertheless, I noticed that "Be the change you wish to see in the world" could be shortened to "Change the world," a personal invitation from Gandhi to me. How could I refuse that? I would just have to work harder to first find and then solve these problems.

Change the world.

Now enlightened, I would try everything, determine shortcomings, and then make a plan. Step-by-step I would fight injustice in the world. Trying everything over my four years was the easy part. I joined speech team for a couple of weeks, got a job tutoring little kids, and another folding clothes for a large retail store. I joined the cross-country and gymnastics teams for my high school. I enjoyed the sports and the friends I made while on the teams, but I wasn't good enough to be a captain. I ran for secretary of my class, but I lost.

As a senior, I began to fill out the standardized Common Application in preparation for college. Everything I had ever done was condensed to a screen on the Internet. It was startling. Almost everything I could have been doing was all found on pull down menus. The common app mocked me for my lack of appointed leadership skills: "I see you ran cross-country. Were you on varsity? No? A captain? No? That's too bad. I'll just leave the rest of this section blank." Screw you, Common App. I worked just as hard as the girls with leadership positions, making sure people felt included on the team, leading the freshmen in long runs around our town; the only difference between us was that they designed the team sweatshirt that everyone was compelled to shell out forty-five dollars for. On their sleeve, "captain so and so" was embroidered; mine was just "so and so." I hated how bitter I felt. I told myself that I had other skills, and I would still get into a dream college, get a perfect education, save the world, and it all would be just fine.

You can't change anything.

But what if your SAT scores weren't what you were expecting them to be?

What if your guidance counselor tells you what you think is a perfect school for you is "a bit" of a reach?

What if you get very sick two weeks before the end of the fall term?

What if that flu results in four incompletes, and that results in the impossibility of your finishing school supplements, and that results in the impossibility of attending your dream school in the fall?

What if you just want everything to stop?

You sit on your sofa a lot. You try to distract yourself with television, but don't really care if that family from North Dakota finds their dream home. Your mother reminds you, gently, "You should try to work on your incompletes." Homework is completed, but not well. Plans made with friends are canceled at the last moment because you're too tired. Apathy is your new favorite emotion, and you do a pretty good job of hiding it. Waitlisted at your dream school, you realize it's not where you wanted to go anyway. But you're still lost. You wish you could get excited for your future, but not knowing exactly what it'll be scares you too much. Caught up in your own thoughts, you're paralyzed. Again, your mother reminds you, much less gently, "Those incompletes will turn into failures if you don't do anything about them." "Okay, mom." You plod through the rest of the year, slowly starting to feel better.

Be the change you wish to see in the world.

Not surprisingly, Gandhi wasn't actually asking me to change the world all by myself. He wasn't even asking me to change the entire world with the help of others. He said exactly what he meant: that all of my actions have meaning, and I should strive for my actions to match with my version of a more perfect world. So even though I wasn't a captain of any sport, by being friendly and welcoming, my actions mirrored how a team should function together. Although I wasn't an elected official on the student board, I still participated at the weekly meetings and ran events for my school. I wasn't obligated to do those things, but did them because I found it enjoyable. With my less than profound re-analyzed version of the quote, by serving the community for joy, I'm changing my world and inspiring others to do the same.

I still have the potential to change the world in the way that Gandhi did. I've got time to determine my passion. I realize it's okay not to know how I'm going to change the world. The high expectations I have for myself are great, but can also be crippling if I don't keep them in check. I know I can leave a positive impact on my community and even the world just by having a positive attitude. I just have to trust that right now I'm already doing exactly what I should be.

The Curse of the Shamrock

GABRIELLE ST PIERRE

In an introduction developed with dialogue, vivid description, rapid character-ization, and iconic imagery, Gabrielle St Pierre captures the tradition-laden characteristics of the Irish side of her family. Richly descriptive and voiced with precise diction, we have much to learn from St Pierre's essay: about celebrating ethnic traditions, about growing into adulthood, and about learning to gain perspective on how precious our contexts are when they are ingrained with love.

"Come in, come in, shut the door behind you, don't let the cold air take the good spirit out!" Six burners on the stove top are all going at once. Mashed potatoes, Shepard's pie, spiral ham, peas with pork, somewhere amidst all the gurgling, boiling, stirring, and simmering, the gravy is burning.

"Hi! How ah' ya?"

"Oh look at my 'Little Man.' He's so big! I think I see a hint of a mustache!"

"You look so cute; I love that sweater. So very festive!"

A Guinness here, a Guinness there; a Lager on the shelf, a Lager on the TV; a Sam Adams by the sofa, a Bud left by the sink.

"It really has been too long."

"I saw you last week!"

"I know, but we need to get together more. We're family."

"We're seeing each other *next* week!"

"NANA! Where's the cheeseball?" Cold air whistles between the many par-tygoers as the door opens and another load of scarves, jackets, and hats are pulled off and thrown on the weary coat stand. They are welcomed in out of the weather (with a familiar reminder to keep the spirits in) and invited into the frenzy with a loud shout from everyone,

"MERRY CHRISTMAS!"

On my mother's side of the family there lies a whole mess of loud and proud Irishmen. As the sign above my nana's front door says, "There are two types of people. Those who are Irish, and those who wish they were." In my family being Irish means more than just wearing green on Saint Patty's day. My family traces "back to County Cork, with the families Cox and O'Brian coming together through Holy Matrimony." This is my grandmother's mantra, her pride in her family lineage never far from her heart or mouth, passed on to her children, grandchildren, and any clerk at the grocery store who compliments her brogue or claddagh ring. In my family, the back door is never locked, plates must always be eaten clean because "our family survived a famine, mind you!" and beer is always in the fridge for every visitor, any time of day. However, the most distinctive, most palpable trait is that my family is all about family.

Being raised within a culture so family-centric means people are forever in your business. There is always a different family member staying at our house, whether they're passing through or have just fallen on hard times. The night before my 13th birthday I slept at my neighbor's house because there weren't enough beds or couches for all the family there to celebrate. At home, people walk in rooms whenever, brush their teeth while you're getting out of the shower, and sing Irish ballads at 2:00 am during finals week. Growing up, I couldn't stand any of it. It was hard enough trying to survive life as a hormonal preteen without everyone watching it happen. There was no way I could try out a new eyeliner, coat, hat, belly shirt, or even t-shirt without someone commenting on the change. I felt constantly observed by the maelstrom of my family. All I wanted was to live how my friends lived. They didn't have to worry about cousins seeing them changing, or never being in the bathroom alone. I envied the fact that they could live their lives independently of everyone else in their family. Their aunts didn't need to know what classes they were taking, whereas mine called to ask why I got a 'B' on my math test! My family felt inescapable, as if I were drowning in the sheer number of their faces, words, and meals. I didn't think I could ever survive it.

I tried my hardest to rebel from the many Irish fists clutching me to their values. Every night it was my mother's tradition to serve dinner at 7:00 pm, and everyone in the house had to come to the table and enjoy the meal together. One day I stopped participating. Instead, I would go eat at a friend's house, or say I was too swamped with homework. If I was forced to sit, I refused to touch a thing, no matter how many times Aunt Sue reminded me of "the great potato famine." My parents were furious that I was so disrespectful and dismissive of the effort they put into each meal. I didn't want them to think of me as such an angry and rebellious teenager, but I couldn't stand the feeling that my life was being controlled by anyone other than me. I wanted to make my own choices so badly, I went as far as to go against my family's long-standing religious traditions. When it came my turn to confirm myself to life following the Catholic Church, I couldn't do it. All I could think about was that I wasn't making this decision for me; I was making it because, in a family with a long religious background, that was what was expected of me. My Mom argued and cried, my cousins tried to explain that confirmation wasn't a big deal, and my Nana swore to everyone that my soul was going right to Hell. In their eyes I was being an immature teenager, making a stubborn decision that would cost me for the rest of my life. All I was really doing was struggling to establish my own identity in a culture that was so ingrained in history and tradition.

When I was younger, this tension between conforming to my family's wishes and trying to break out and be my own person was at the forefront of my everyday life. Now, I don't see any of them…EVER! In college I can eat when I want, sleep when I want, and I don't have to get anyone's permission. Surprisingly enough, now that I have what I've always wanted I am truly starting to appreciate all that I had. I am thankful that I know how to make an army of crisply sheeted beds, that I'm used to living with people around me all day and night, that I know how to welcome guests, and that I know how to make a mean cheeseball. As I'm meeting people from all different walks of life, I'm appreciating the love my family always gave me, and truly respecting our traditions and heritage. (Hey! Didn't you know? Surviving a famine is no small thing!) Now, I've finally come to accept the second saying on my Nana's door: "You can pick your friends, but you can't pick your family."

I'll welcome them with hugs, kisses, and reminders to shut the door and keep the good spirits in. I'll have six burners going on the stovetop, and I'll have to shoo all the little kids away from the ham. I'll always end up burning the gravy. Everyone will chat, drink, laugh, and make up bawdy lyrics to Christmas carols. I'll be everyone's favorite Nana when I bring out the cheeseball. Each person who puts a foot over my threshold will be greeted with a deep cheer because whether related by blood, marriage, friendship, sports clubs, or bar stools, they are all family, and for that one Christmas day, they are all considered Irish.

Interacting with Text

Preface

We often write to engage with the ideas of others, particularly in academic contexts. Because dialogue is at the heart of meaning-making in universities, *College Writing* asks students to "wrestle" with a published text in a unit called "Interacting with Text." Writing to an academic audience, students work to balance understanding and fair representation of the text (specifically, effective summary, paraphrase, quotation, and citation of a text) with a critical response. This begins the process of writing to more distant audiences—audiences that are broader than fellow classmates, family members, or friends—and to understand the kinds of thinking and writing valued by academic communities.

The "Interacting with Text" essays included here represent student interactions with the work of published writers. Drawing on their own histories and experiences, these student writers place their own perspectives in dialogue with those of a published writer. The challenge is, at once, to contemplate the sophisticated ideas shared by professional authors in the course's reader and to present one's own perspective on those ideas: for example, to re-think one's perspective on the topic, to apply a writer's claims to a different context, to tease apart the nuances of a writer's assertions, to re-define a key concept in an essay, and more. To understand these writers' ways of responding, we might imagine how the writers of the "Inquiring into Self" essays, based on their personal contexts, might have responded differently to the issues presented in this section.

The Truth Behind Tourism

SARAH KATZ

Sarah Katz bases her response to Jamaica Kincaid's "A Small Place" upon her own experience with tourism in Salem, MA, and working at a yacht club. Katz's reader-response approach takes her audience along her own journey through Kincaid's essay. Note her use of empathy, pathos, and rhetorical analysis to arrive at a deeper understanding of Kincaid than where she initially began.

If you had asked me what I thought about tourists a few weeks ago, I would have answered briefly, basing my response on my experience with the busy streets and crowded sidewalks in Salem, Massachusetts during the month of October. I would have said that the large influx of people makes a simple, five-minute errand consume a far longer amount of time. I would not even think about tourists on a tropical island since I have never had the chance to be one of those vacationers. I had never thought about how a native of a struggling island would feel about tourists to their homeland, and I'm sure many other people like me have overlooked considering what their lives are like. Of course, I have always known that tropical islands are popular spots for vacationing, but it never occurred to me how harmful a tourist could really be until reading Jamaica Kincaid's essay, "A Small Place."

In her essay, Kincaid analyzes a tourist from her viewpoint as a native of a third world country. She takes her readers through a "typical" tropical island vacation, outlining the naiveté and ignorance of many individuals. Reading "A Small Place" opened my eyes to the selfish attitude of a tourist. In order to get her points across, Kincaid chooses to generalize and stereotype tourists as "ugly people." Although Kincaid's tone of voice is harsh, critical, and even rude at some points, her essay succeeds in addressing the issues raised by tourists visiting third world country islands. A tourist simply does not realize the mental and emotional toll they have on a native, as well as the amount that they take for granted while vacationing on these islands.

After my first reading of Kincaid's essay, I admit that I was offended by her description of a tourist in Antigua. I wondered why Kincaid thought she had the right to call someone like me ugly. And why should a tourist have to worry about the issues of an Antiguan? I now realize that this is the exact point that Kincaid is making about people who come to Antigua. We are all too selfish to even try to understand the constant battle for food and money that some islanders must go through every day. Even though I have never traveled to Antigua, or any other island, I assume that if I had before reading "A Small Place," my vacation would be much like the one she describes. The thought of being an island native, struggling day to day, might cross my mind, but it most likely would not have an impact on my time away from home. Most people would have the same experience since they would not know what some people must do simply to survive.

Initially, I was insulted when Kincaid started to use unappealing descriptions to make her points. "An ugly thing, that is what you are when you become a tourist, an ugly, empty thing…" (116). I understand that a tourist can look unintelligent merely by marveling at every little thing, but this is not the point Kincaid is trying to make. She is not referring to my physical appearance or that of any other vacationer. It is the way we are able to lounge carelessly on the white sand right in front of island natives who may never get a chance to be a tourist in a foreign country. Poor island natives cannot stand us because we are a constant reminder of the lives they do not have. I am not saying Kincaid and other natives want to live like us. I am sure they do not after I consider how bizarrely we act, day after day, while on vacation. Instead, I believe that we make their lives more difficult simply by existing in their country.

In order to understand this essay, we need to put ourselves in Kincaid's place and try to imagine living her life. After thinking about the differing lives of a tourist and a struggling island native, I realized that it is a form of envy that takes place within the Antiguans described in "A Small Place." It is not jealousy since Kincaid makes it very clear that "they laugh at your strangeness," and "the physical sight of you does not please them" (116). It is clear that she does not want to be like a tourist. The island natives simply envy the fact that people can come to their island whenever they feel like leaving home, and make the place in which they struggle a wonderful place of enjoyment. How could they not envy these tourists?

Although I do not come close when being compared to an Antiguan, I think that I can understand what one might feel towards tourists based on my experience of working at a yacht club. It is not that I didn't like the members of the yacht club; I simply envied them. While they were allowed to lounge around and eat fancy meals sitting next to the ocean, I was busy carrying heavy trays, working long hours, and picking up after them in order to make money. No, I did not depend on my paycheck to feed my family, and I'm sure this work is nothing compared to the work some Antiguans must do, but there was still that feeling of envy inside me. The club members seemed to be on vacation every single day, attending cocktail parties and going on boat rides. They were an entirely different group of people in my eyes. Of course, this is not nearly as extreme as an Antiguan catering to a tourist, but I believe that the same feeling occurs within both situations.

Before reading this essay, I could not fathom the number of items and necessities I constantly take for granted. I wasn't living in a bubble, unaware of the rest of the world, but it was hard to know what some have to do for the simple things that are readily available to me and not of concern in my life. "You must not wonder what exactly happened to the contents of your lavatory when you flushed it. You must not wonder where your bathwater went when you pulled out the stopper" (115). Even if a tourist were educated on the plumbing system in Antigua, they still wouldn't have to live with it. After all, they are going home to some place more developed. By listing these processes that are concerning in Antigua, Kincaid points out that a tourist *wouldn't* wonder about these things because he or she does not understand life without development. This is what makes a tourist ignorant—the fact that they would not wonder or worry about these complexities because they are unaffected by them back home.

If you can get past Kincaid's critical tone of voice presented in "A Small Place," you can truly understand the main issues she is pointing out about tourists in her essay. And you will realize that the harsh tone is necessary to make readers understand the issues taking place on third world country islands. In order for change to occur, you must first be willing to step outside of your world and see life through the eyes of someone much, much less fortunate: someone who values every little crumb and penny. Then, you must imagine someone flaunting their wealth in front of you, thinking that your home, with its undeveloped plumbing and unpaved roads, is a wonderful environment. Without understanding the difficulty you are putting an Antiguan through by living a typical tourist life, you cannot feel their pain as they watch you relax on their suffering island.

I was much like the typical tourist described in this essay just a few weeks ago. I did not understand why a tourist should even have to think about someone else's difficulties while they are on vacation, trying to get away from their own issues. I was the exact person Kincaid targets in her essay. I am now aware of why and how a tourist complicates the lives of island natives even further. Jamaica Kincaid's essay "A Small Place" may have been insulting to read at first, but it changed my view on tourism, and that is exactly what she intended to do.

Work Cited

Kincaid, Jamaica. "A Small Place." *Other Words: A Writer's Reader.* Eds. David Fleming et al. Dubuque: Kendall Hunt, 2009. 111–116. Print.

Feminization, Education, Masculinity: A Response to Michael S. Kimmel

ANDY MARTON

Between the epigrammatic quotes that structure his essay and a distinctive voice that is all his own, Andy Marton illustrates how to respond fairly to another author while making an original argument in a unique framework. Marton represents Kimmel's points without losing his own voice among the quotes. Rather, he extends Kimmel's points while testing them against his own experiences in high school, with family, and in his personal relationships.

Because there is very little honor left in American life, there is a certain built-in tendency to destroy masculinity in American men.
—**Norman Mailer**

In, "'What About the Boys?' What the Current Debates Tell Us—and Don't Tell Us—About Boys in School," Michael S. Kimmel cites the statistic that boys "commit suicide four times more often than girls; they get into fights twice as often; they murder ten times more frequently and are 15 times more likely to be the victims of a violent crime" (91–92). His article examines why we have these disturbing figures. After reading his essay and reflecting upon my own experiences as a boy, I came to a conclusion similar to his: that boys in America are being trained with too much machismo that separates our "manliness" from our humanity.

Let's start with the claim that boys are being feminized. It sounds like this: in a world of political correctness and feminine idealism run amok, there is nowhere left for boys to assert their natural manliness and aggression. They're forced to act against their instincts, and the frustration of this unnatural abomination builds up with no healthy outlet for them. Kimmel rejects this idea by stating that it "creates a false opposition between girls and boys" (94). By arguing about why boys are so out of control, how they're neglected, we make the false assumption that girls and boys are completely different creatures and that there is nothing they have in common, an idea that Kimmel calls insulting (106).

I agree with Kimmel. Feminism has always been challenged, and its critics are willing to pervert it to re-assert male dominance. Reading Kimmel's portrayal of these arguments, I get from anti-feminist critics a call to return to the days where "men could be men" and women "knew their place," perhaps as docile housewives. I grew uncomfortable reading these arguments because they made me feel that women and girls are the enemy, the eternal yin to our yang, a force to be diminished. They didn't make me feel that women are human beings.

Having your adolescence at an all-male boarding school is just crap.
                                                        —Benedict Cumberbatch

This brings me to the conflict over single-sex education. If we accept the idea that boys and girls are irreconcilably different, then it seems reasonable to explore the option of creating schools for boys and schools for girls. It does seem, on the face of things, like an ideal arrangement. In my junior year of high school, I barely scraped by with a 'C' for the year in physics because I took it with my then-girlfriend. I didn't focus, and we'd sometimes sneak out of the class for a while. It would be easy to make the argument that I would have done better academically in an all-boys school.

Kimmel rejects this idea. He asserts that "women's colleges may constitute a challenge to gender inequality, while men's colleges reproduce that inequality" (102). In short, men are taught that women are inferior to them because where are the women to say otherwise? Kimmel also declares that "single-sex education for women often perpetuates detrimental attitudes and stereotypes about women" (103). Essentially, these colleges reinforce gender stereotypes. One of my friends goes to the all-female Smith College, which is known for its liberal arts education, as is Mount Holyoke. Meanwhile, the very math-and-science based schools are heavily male. CalTech reported 65% of incoming students in 2013 were male, and M.I.T. reported that in 2014 55% of those admitted were male.

I, however, think single-sex colleges are more an effect of stereotyping rather than a cause; by the time students get to college, gender seems to have divided students on school subjects. According to the article, high school boys tended to list science and math as their favorite subjects, while girls listed the humanities, citing their genders as reasons why (Kimmel 101). Math is a "male subject" because it's concrete, while English, where there is no one right answer, and everyone is free to share various thoughts, feelings, and interpretations, is seen as feminine. It's easier to reinforce stereotypes about what subject goes with what gender when the boys and girls are kept apart from each other.

I have two observations about separate-sex facilities to add to Kimmel's. The first is that arguments for these facilities are rooted in the idea that everyone is heterosexual. Some estimates conclude that ten percent of the population—which is not negligible—is homosexual. They are not being served by a school that is supposed to take dating pressures away from them.

The other observation I had was that whatever problems men seem to have interacting with women (and vice-versa) are just that, problems. The answer isn't separating boys and girls because we distract each other. That's not how life works. Dealing with the opposite sex is a learned ability. I stated before that because I took physics with my girlfriend, I got a "C" for the year. Dating a classmate doesn't justify a bad grade. My dad (who married his high school sweetheart) was furious when I tried to make that my excuse. If there really is such a problem between boys and girls regarding how they interact around each other, however, then it's better to teach in school how to resolve that tension rather than to increase it. I'm convinced that single-sex schools do the latter, exacerbating this supposed rift rather than healing it.

Boys will be boys—Unknown (common expression)

So feminization isn't the problem. Coeducational schools aren't the problem. What is the problem? Could it be cultural? Could it be biological? Why is it, as Kimmel points out, that "few European nations would boast of such violent, homophobic, and misogynist adolescent males" (99–100), while the U.S. has all these scary statistics? I've grown up always hearing that boys are just like that naturally—they just normally lean towards aggression and violence. It's biological. Our testosterone just makes us want to run around, hit things, act "like a boy." But aggression is not biological or hereditary. Kimmel cites a study from Stanford that shows that testosterone "doesn't cause it [aggression], but it does facilitate and enable the aggression that's already there" (96). So, aggression has to come from somewhere else.

I've always thought it to be cultural. In America, we're bombarded with aggression and violence. Football is one of the most popular games in American culture. Our superheroes use their might to beat up or kill the bad guys. All of us are taught the basic "boy code" that Kimmel summarizes in the essay: don't be a sissy (I heard that one a lot growing up), fight to be in charge, and take risks (99). I don't know why in America we have such a focus on boys having to act like this. Or why it's encouraged. Whenever I got too rowdy or aggressive, or too macho (my parents' favorite word when I exhibited a bit too much of this behavior), my mother's first words were always, "Don't be a dumbass." She and my father always say that this need for aggression to prove how manly you are is stupid, especially when it results in games like "Flinch" that Kimmel describes (105).

Not only is it stupid, it's dangerous. Part of childhood is learning control. It's not necessarily a good thing when a boy is aggressive. The right response is to find better ways of channeling, not encouraging these feelings, as therapist Michael Gurian would have us do (Kimmel 107).

I attended Wayland High School, which, in 2011, underwent a serious tragedy. We had a student at my school who had always been aggressive and violent. He played football and was very good at it. Once in a while, he was known to have a violent outburst or a tantrum, but hey, what boy doesn't lose his temper once in a while? When his girlfriend broke up with him, he was upset, but he didn't share his feelings. Why would he? That's sissy stuff. The summer after they graduated, he brutally beat his former girlfriend and strangled her to death with a Bungee cord. He's currently in prison serving life without parole. But the most chilling part of this story is that everyone was shocked he could do this. Why? "Well, sure, he had a temper, but that's just normal." While he is responsible for what he did, isn't it possible that not encouraging violence and aggression in boys the way our culture does could have prevented this young woman's tragic death?

I'm not just a boy toy. I have feelings and dreams like anybody else.
—Jon Stewart

This quote highlights my overall point. The problem isn't that boys' natural aggression is being held back; it's that we live in a society where boys have this culture of "manliness" thrust upon them very early in their lives that's so unhealthy. I feel bombarded all the time with the cultural need to prove my dominance over other men, and especially over women. That's a sentiment that I find to be deeply harmful.

I could spend several more pages talking about possible sources for boys' aggression—abusive fathers, our media, fear of being perceived as gay, Freudian penis envy—but it doesn't matter. We know that there is some problem with boys when they murder, commit suicide, drop out, and suffer from depression at staggering rates. As we've seen, I reject the idea that feminism or coeducation has caused these problems. In fact, my argument lies in that both are good things. Growing up, we all (boys and girls) need to be encouraged to become human beings: good people who don't need to use violence to express themselves, who aren't afraid to show emotion at appropriate moments. Kimmel ends his essay with this declaration: "Feminists also seem to believe the outrageous proposition that, if given enough love, compassion, and support, boys—as well as men—can also be people. That's a vision of boyhood I believe is worth fighting for" (107). I couldn't agree more.

Andy Marton

Works Cited

"2013 Incoming Class Profile." *CalTech Undergraduate Admissions*. n.d. Web. 04 Oct. 2013.

Kimmel, Michael S. "'What About the Boys?' What the Current Debates Tell Us—And Don't Tell Us—About Boys in School." *Other Words: A Writer's Reader*. Eds. David Fleming et al. Dubuque: Kendall Hunt, 2009. 91–110. Print.

"Massachusetts Institute of Technology." *US News & World Report*. n.d. Web. 04 Oct. 2013.

Analizar Anzaldúa/Analyzing Anzaldúa

LOUISE MONROE

Another essay that employs form to structure her argument, Louise Monroe's reading of Gloria Anzaldúa uses bilingual headings to reflect Anzaldúa's own focus on border culture. Monroe's rhetorical analysis does not shy away from translating Spanish, and largely focuses on the pathos that Anzaldúa evokes. Both Anzaldúa and Monroe's essays exemplify how writing can lead to a new understanding of the world and our place in it, particularly at places such as the borderland where language, space, culture, and history converge.

As young children we were taught that Christopher Columbus was responsible for our very existence. The United States would not have existed without his heroic efforts. Yet, around sixth grade, it began to let slip that that wasn't *exactly* how colonization happened. The happy picture of the New World settlers and the original Native Americans residents joining together as one in joyful unity was far from the truth. It wasn't as if the two cultures were sitting around the campfire telling jokes. The Europeans treated the Native Americans horribly, taking over their land and killing off their population.

This unequal partnership of cultures was mirrored in many places around the Americas. Westward expansion and the pursuit of "manifest destiny" led to the demolition of many cultures that were different from that of the expansionists. The current United States-Mexican border continues to be affected by the past terrors of the colonists and continued persecution by the United States. In her essay "The Homeland, Atzlán / El otro México," Gloria Anzaldúa creates an intriguing account of the history and personal struggle of the people who live on the border of the United States and Mexico. Perhaps even more intriguing than the actual story she spins is the way she spins it. Anzaldúa is an authorial powerhouse, commanding her audience to *listen!* "Pay attention to me," she demands through her rhetoric, a siren with a pen. Even though the piece is simply being read, it appeals to many senses and emotions. Auditory and memory skills, in addition to one's ability to read, are all called to attention. One is pushed to use all of his or her capabilities when studying this piece.

Escuchar/Listen

"El otro México que acá hemos construido el espacio es lo que ha sido territorio nacional" (39) roughly translates to: "The other Mexico that we have constructed / over there [in the U.S.] is in a place that was once / our [Mexico's] national territory." The "other Mexico" is the land the white people took over as they continuously pushed back the Mexican-United States border. The authors of this quotation, Los Tigros del Norte, as noted in Anzaldúa's footnote, are what is known as a *conjunto* band. Conjunto music originated during the 1800s in this border area that Anzaldúa knows so well. It has infiltrated both sides of the border to reach the people who are most affected by the barbwire. The music is a large part of the culture of the people; thus Anzaldúa chose to begin her essay with a verse from a *conjunto* song. Later she blends Spanish with English as she points out the dangers of trying to cross the border. "¿Qué dicen muchachos a echársela de mojado?" translates to "What do you say, guys/brothers, about crossing over?" (47). The answers they must entertain are not easy. The conversation continues, pointing to the great risk immigrant people take when trying to cross the border: the possibility of facing a coyote or dangers of another kind—having to depend on a drug or other kind of smuggler or being entrapped into cheap labor by "recruiters." The border is one without an element of safety ("Texas").

Both of these inclusions bring a traditional element of culture to the piece. Instances of culture which began and are dominant on the Mexican side of the border show that these people are their own people. They should be able to have a place to call home. They aren't just a smattering of nomads, all randomly brought together. They are a people who have persisted through generations, united as one, to maintain a culture they are so desperately trying to keep alive against the oppression of the white intruders. Their culture is as real as their struggle for survival. They are not simply the white people's throwaways.

Anzaldúa uses English and Spanish language throughout her piece. The text is created primarily for an English-speaking audience: the American people. Yet, the bits of intertwined Spanish are effective in proving her argument. The language strengthens the way she creates this border culture for the reader. In the first poem of the piece, she mentions "the sea" in English, yet in the next line refers to it as "el mar" (40). The inclusion of both shows how her culture, lands, even her nature are split by the "1,950 mile-long wound / dividing a *pueblo*, a culture, / running down the length of my body..." (40), as she refers to the border fence separating Mexico from America. Instead of calling the people originally from Texas, "Texans," she refers to them as "Tejanos," their true, original name. This border culture is one in which the white American people are dominant, and the native people are the subordinates. The balance of power becomes one of inequality, crooked. These people are reflections of the constant tug-of-war of the land, and the use of both languages presents an expression of this. The uniquely tragic cultural relationship between these two groups has been formed through the continual conquest and terror occurring throughout history. The border culture that has been created is strained due to one group's personal entitlement complex: the residents of the United States believe they are a superior strain of people.

The incorporations of Spanish language reinforce a stronger credibility to Anzaldúa as an author as well as adding to the strength of the piece. It adds to the realism that she actually is a person of border culture. As she tells how she has been personally affected by these misfortunes (i.e. her father had to switch professions from a farmer to a sharecropper because large corporations forced the end of dry land farming in the border area), one can more readily become a believer of the story and events that have taken place. The language hopscotch shows she is a person of both Mexico and the United States—that she is a child of injustice.

Escribir/Write

The poetry passages are arguably the best portion of the piece. Beginning with her own words, each passage conveys true emotion, adding to her central argument. By placing the poetry at the start of the essay, she can easily draw the reader in, an effective authorial technique. She chooses not to begin with an immediate attack on the white American counterparts who have made her and her people's lives so miserable. No, she chooses an emotional angle to tell her story. The words, "I stand at the edge where earth touches ocean / where the two overlap / a gentle coming together / at other times and places a violent clash," (39) lie within the first stanza. Soft words such as "gentle" and "touches" contrast with the "violent clash," as beginning descriptors between the innocence of the native people in opposition with the forcefulness of those who took over.

I believe one of the most compelling and powerful lines, not only in this poem but in the entire piece, comes a few stanzas before the end of this particular poem: "This is my home / this thin edge of / barbwire" (40). This statement epitomizes the whole inner struggle of these people. They have been pushed back and forth against the wire (figuratively and literally), too many times to count. Their home has become nothing—nothing, but a thin, sharp, cold piece of wire—strong enough to force the separation of the two nations and cultures. But most importantly, it has created a terrible sense of isolation. This isolation has made the people into a lower class and forced them to abide by the United States' pressure to stay within their boundaries. Their economy and way of life are controlled almost entirely by the white forces controlling their land. The people have become a product of this wire, weary and frustrated. The barbwire has become home. A home unlike any most of us will be able to imagine in our posh, easy lives. This is no land with a corresponding jingle confirming that yes, this land is my land, and this land is your land. No. These people have not felt such cheerfulness about their home in a long time.

Anzaldúa continues the essay by incorporating more poetry, but from other authors. These poems are further reflections by authors explaining, interpreting, and remembering the oppression of their people and the current border culture issues. This works as a technique because it provides more evidence than just Anzaldúa's own opinions and research. For example, author Violeta Parra is included: "El indio se cae muerto, y el afuerino de pie," remarks on the "Lost Land" of the Indian people: "The Indian falls dead, / and the outsider is left standing (43). The land is no longer one to call his or her own.

Recordar/Remember

Anzaldúa remarks on the history of the people of the land many years back. She describes the first people who lived on the land, tracing back to the roots of those who first called this place home. She chronologically describes each event which has led to today's reality: the battles, the economic changes, the unrecognized treaties, and so on. She relates back to the Aztec people not only by describing how they came to the border area, but also how they are believed to have arrived spiritually. She does this by inserting a small poem describing Huitzilopochtli, the God of War—"los aztecas siguieron al dios Huitzilopochtli," or in English, "The Aztecs followed the god / Huizilopochtli" (42). She thus incorporates a deep native cultural belief into her piece. After describing this folk tale, she starts an account of how Hernan Cortes and the Spaniards conquered the land and killed over fifteen million of the native people. By describing beliefs of an ancient culture and then paralleling it to the people who were ultimately responsible for the death and demise of many of the native people, Anzaldúa creates emotion. The current European views of the conquests are often thought of with pride: they gained land. However, through Anzaldúa's account, these advances are described not as a success but as a slaughter.

If she had chosen just to use her own opinions, the essay might be weak. By using factual evidence as well as other literary texts, she shows that she is not the only one seeing this as an issue—so do many other people. In addition to her factual evidence, Anzaldúa creates a very strong emotional piece as well. Her strength as a writer provides an argument so compelling, it is impossible for the reader to ignore. The combination of factual and emotional language and evidence create an undeniably strong essay. The techniques and strategies Anzaldúa uses strengthen her piece to perfect a mixing of pathos and logos to form ethos. The rhetoric is intellectually impeccable.

Work Cited

Anzaldúa, Gloria. "The Homeland, Aztlán / El otro México." *Other Words: A Writer's Reader*. Eds. David Fleming et al. Dubuque: Kendall Hunt, 2009. 39–49. Print.

The Temptations of an Addict

LINDA NGUYEN

*Linda Nguyen roots her response to Kurt Vonnegut's essay "1983: New York,"
which argues that U.S. leaders are addicted to preparing for war, in her personal
context of watching her father grapple with his addiction to cigarettes. While
Nguyen acknowledges that the scope of these addictions is very different, they
nevertheless affect the people surrounding the addict in the same way: Nguyen's
frustrated family stands in for Vonnegut's annoyed nation. Nguyen uses quotes
and paraphrase to assert her own voice.*

The day that my grandfather was diagnosed with lung cancer was the day
that my dad decided to quit smoking his cigarettes. Maybe it was his fear of
dying early that made him stop, or his respect for his father, but on that day,
he was sure that he could give up his old habit and start anew. Dad threw out
his half empty carton of Marlboro reds and went to the nearest pharmacy to
pick up some nicotine patches. The entire family was overjoyed, and we all did
our utmost to support him. Unfortunately, this decision of his only lasted for
about two weeks. Like so many of his past "no smoking" resolutions, this one
eventually fell to temptation, and his attempt was shortly abandoned. Dad
had an addiction to smoking.

An addiction can be a very dangerous thing. In the article "1983: New York"
by Kurt Vonnegut, the author compares the severity of an addiction to preparing for war to that of the addiction of an alcoholic or gambler. He writes:

> I now wish to call attention to another form of addiction, which has not
> been previously identified. It is more like gambling than drinking, since
> people afflicted are ravenous for situations that will cause their bodies to
> release exciting chemicals into their bloodstreams. I am persuaded that
> there are among us people who are tragically hooked on preparations for
> war (Vonnegut 297).

Smoking, drinking, gambling, and preparing for war are all controversial
subjects—when abused, these vices can destroy. The author's main objective
within the passage is to criticize the fact that addiction to preparing for war
is not looked at as a bad habit, when in retrospect, its effects can be more

devastating than the effects of an alcohol or gambling addiction. Vonnegut also proposes that in order to resolve a problem, one must be able to admit that there is a problem in the first place; this may be the hardest barrier to fixing the problem.

With Dad, it was not until he saw the effects of Grandpa's smoking that he was able to understand that his addiction would lead him to a similarly tragic end. It took him 27 years of smoking cigarettes to realize this, but even after he realized that he needed to stop smoking, he was not able to follow through with the decision due to his lack of resolve; it is always easier for people to think about taking action than to actually take action.

Vonnegut mentions this assumption in his article when he refers to the temptations of a hypothetical alcoholic president, who knows for a fact that "if he took just one more drink, the whole planet would blow up" (299). And when this president is directly in the presence of alcohol, Vonnegut asks, "What do you think he'll do?" (299). His question indirectly illustrates the uncertainty of war when in the midst of addiction. Vonnegut also leaves the answer open ended in order to stimulate the thoughts of the readers and raise concerns as to the real consequences of war. Through his portrayal of the inescapable lure of addiction, he illustrates that it is difficult to overcome and satisfy.

In his essay, Vonnegut argues that addiction to preparing for war should be treated in the same manner that addiction to other substances should be treated: those addicted must be willing to admit that they have a problem and proactively try to resolve it. When Dad first acknowledged that he had a problem, the family was ecstatic—not because we thought that he would immediately quit smoking—we knew better than to hope for that. What was important for the family was that Dad acknowledged his problem. Many times beforehand, Dad had been cajoled and guilt-tripped into quitting. "This family is full of naggers," he used to say. And with every half-hearted attempt he made, we were graced with disappointing results and a grumpy father. Every failed attempt made us more numb to his addiction; it would be brought up in conversation occasionally in a joking manner, but we all believed that it was an insurmountable problem. This is why when Dad took initiative to end his addiction, we had cause for celebration. At least he knew that there were possible measures that he could take to stop his addiction. Throughout the essay, Vonnegut illustrates the struggles of both alcoholics and gamblers in order to compare the symptoms of addiction with those of people addicted to the thrill of preparing for war. He uses the comparisons in order to condemn the nation's thirst for conflict. Vonnegut attempts to advocate for peace instead of violence, using his writing as a tool to protest the warmongering nature of the world.

Addictions are difficult to overcome, but removing the desire for warfare is a nearly impossible feat. Dad's problem can be fixed; his smoking addiction is one that he can conquer with enough willpower and self-control. However, Vonnegut's writing suggests that the problem of war is much bigger and will not be able to be solved:

> If we know a compulsive gambler who is dead broke, we can probably make him happy with a dollar to bet on who can spit farther than some-one else. For us to give a compulsive war-preparer a fleeting moment of happiness, we may have to buy him three Trident submarines and a hundred intercontinental ballistic missiles mounted on choo-choo trains. (298)

Vonnegut's prose suggests that unlike smoking and gambling, an addiction to warfare involves much larger ramifications and will never truly be satisfied. War and the thirst for it are global problems involving numerous cultures and traditions from all around the world. Vonnegut proposes that mankind must attempt to change in order to rid the world of its thirst for war and violence. He also challenges whether or not this idea of his is even possible. Violence has been ingrained into our culture. Mortal conflicts ever since the dawn of time have always been solved with violence. Warfare is synchronous with human nature, so how does one attempt to separate being human and having a thirst for conflict? Vonnegut also informs the readers that war is a serious matter that can be compared to addiction, but with more dire consequences. Even when Dad took the steps to quit smoking, he could not cure himself of his addiction. If one man cannot quit smoking, how can entire societies cure themselves of the addiction to war?

Although Dad realized the severity of his addiction, he has never been able to quit smoking, no matter how hard he has tried. The temptation of the relief that he gets from a single cigarette will forever keep him hooked. People too are hooked on the idea of going to war. Vonnegut's writing illustrates the heart of addiction and criticizes the nature of humankind and its strong taste for violence.

Work Cited

Vonnegut, Kurt. "1983: New York." *Other Words: A Writer's Reader.* Eds. David Fleming et al. Dubuque: Kendall Hunt, 2009. 297–299. Print.

May I Borrow Your Pen?

ARIANNA WILLS

Arianna Wills directly borrows the form of George Saunders' "The Braindead Megaphone" in her rhetorical analysis of his essay. She considers how Saunders' rhetoric figures his relationship to his audience and the implications for that stance, even as she herself makes the same moves.

1. In my tenth grade chemistry class, my teacher handed out an article entitled "The Dangers of Dihydrogen Monoxide." The article was an in-depth look at this mystery chemical infecting pretty much everything in our lives. A lot of kids were getting kind of freaked out while my teacher just got more and more smug. Turns out Dihyrdrogen (as in two hydrogens) Monoxide (as in one oxygen) was H2O, as in water. This sensationalist piece of writing was warning about the dangers of plain old water. Basically, the article was a joke, a scam, a piece of propaganda to warn against people falling into the trap of believing whatever they hear. My teacher went on to say that at one point the piece had been read on the radio as a joke, and the radio hosts nearly got arrested for disturbing the peace.

The way information is presented to us determines the way we perceive it. The article on Dihydrogen Monoxide was written like a reputable source, like a science article with a lot of scientific-sounding words to back it up and make it believable. If the article had been presented initially as being about water then no one would have taken it seriously. Bottom line is this: rhetoric is important to how an audience receives and understands a piece of information.

2. In the essay "The Braindead Megaphone," George Saunders' goal is to have his audience understand that the nature of the news media can be dangerous and shows how the quality of what it presents has been disintegrating over the past few decades. He also wants his readers to question the validity and the objectivity of the news media—the way it presents stories, and why and how it chooses its stories. He is very careful not to alienate his readers in any way through his use of voice and diction. He also keeps his readers interested and helps them understand his arguments by using storytelling as well

as hypothetical and real life examples. Saunders also makes his essay easier for the reader's mind to digest by breaking it up into small numbered mini-chapters. His use of formatting within those chapters aids the audience in following the logical progression of the essay. Saunders convinces his readers to actively think about and question the news media that American society has come to accept in ways they ordinarily would not.

3. Imagine this: you are talking to a robot. The robot does not talk like a human with a human voice; it talks like a robot. It uses disturbingly correct grammar and the word 'illogical' a lot. It is talking *at* you instead of *to* you. The robot's lack of humanity is a barrier between you and what is being said, and you have to stand on your tip toes to see over that barrier. This situation is difficult, mildly irritating, and you really want to stop having a conversation with this robot. And, since this is a metaphor, and the robot is really an essay written to a perfection that is stiff and inhuman, you can and do stop reading.

An essay should aim to do at least two things: make you want to continue reading it and make you think critically about what is being said. If its author is talking to you like a human being and is making an effort to help you understand something by speaking in a way you understand, odds are you are going to keep listening.

4. Saunders writes as though he is having a conversation; he keeps his voice casual while still having carefully constructed, sophisticated thoughts. He continually includes himself in the audience by using "we" and "us," and by doing so, he avoids making his audience feel accused or attacked. For example, when talking about America's rush into the Iraqi war, he starts to sound as if his purpose is to advance an anti-war position:

> What had gone dead was the curious part that should have been helping us *decide* about the morality and intelligence of invasion, that should have known that the war being discussed was a real war, that might actually happen, to real, currently living people. Where was our sense of agonized wondering, of real doubt? We got (to my memory) a lot of discussion of tactics (which route, which vehicles) and strategy (how would it "play on the Arab street") but not much about the essential morality of invasion (Saunders 242).

This sentiment appears to be anti-war, but before he can alienate his pro-war readership, he moves on quickly, tempering his position: "Am I oversimplifying here? Yes. Is all our media stupid? Far from it. […] But: is some of our media very stupid? Hoo boy. Does stupid, near-omnipresent media make us more tolerant toward stupidity in general? It would be surprising if it didn't" (Saunders 242). Saunders moves on before his readership can get bogged down in the anti-Iraq war sentiments, and he avoids causing a stir among those readers who might disagree with his opinion by pushing the reader back to his original point: the media's shallowness and irresponsibility. He tucks his opinion on the war into his argument, but in order to avoid losing part of his audience, he does not linger on the subject.

An example of his self-insertion into the text, as well as his humor that serves him well throughout the essay, comes later when talking about the average nightly newscast:

> Last night on the local news I watched a young reporter standing in front of our mall, obviously freezing his ass off. The essence of his report was, Malls Tend to Get Busier at Christmas! Then he reported the local implications of his investigations: (1) This Also True at Our Mall! (2) When Our Mall More Busy, More Cars Present in Parking Lot! (3) The More Cars, the Longer It Takes Shoppers to Park! and (shockingly): (4) Yet People Still Are Shopping, Due to, It Is Christmas! (Saunders 242)

Saunders uses an example he witnessed and makes it funny by reducing the story to its barest parts, showing us how common sense the story is, and how it really has no place on the daily news. Saunders goes onto say:

> Across our fair city, people sat there and took it, and I believe that, generally, they weren't laughing at him either. They, like us in our house, were used to it, and consented to the idea that some Informing had just occurred. Although what we had been told, we already knew [...] we took it, and, I would say, it did something to us: made us dumber and more accepting of slop. (242)

Saunders groups himself with those who accepted the bogus news story about the level of busyness at the mall in order to avoid pointing fingers. He puts himself on the same playing field as his audience, thereby making him more available to the audience, easier to relate to, and easier to listen to. Saunders attempts to make his audience aware of what the media is doing and how they, the audience, are reacting to it. By blaming himself as well as his readers, he blames society as a whole. He avoids being accusatory and is instead able to convey that we are all in this together, which implies that society as a collective can also change the media. Therefore he is deflecting direct blame and implying that there is hope for change at the same time. By keeping his tone casual and by including himself in the text, he makes himself more available to the reader. He also achieves this through his diction. By combining complex language and casual language with a casual voice, he creates a persona that is both intellectual and easily understood by a wide range of readers. He intrigues the audience with humor and storytelling while remaining both accessible and intelligent. By doing this he appeals to scholarly readers and non-scholarly readers alike.

5. I'm going to tell you a story. Are you interested? Did that catch you a little bit? Of course it did. Stories are interesting. Whether they are true or fictional, a story holds a captivating curiosity for humans—like a laser pointer for a cat. Now, I am sure there is some deep-rooted psychological and anthropological reasoning behind the human desire to hear stories. But the bottom line is that people love them. People love gossip, stories, fantasies. They are interesting little escapes from reality, and they make us think: Is it true? What does it all mean? So when someone offers to tell you a story, well now you are listening.

6. Saunders' relaxed tone also lends itself to another important aspect of his writing—his storytelling. Saunders plays on people's natural desire to hear stories, and using that to his advantage, he makes important points with the use of hypothetical scenarios. His use of storytelling helps to captivate the reader which helps him make his point. Saunders typically starts by building a relatively simple scenario, i.e. "imagine a party," and then proceeds to build upon that simple scenario and make it more complex while keeping it easy to understand (239). For example, in the party scenario, Saunders sets up a typical party and then he adds the guy with the megaphone. The guy with the megaphone starts talking to the partygoers, and the partygoers listen and eventually respond to what he is saying, whether they had initially intended to or not (Saunders 240). Saunders goes onto explain: "These responses are predicated not on his intelligence, his unique experience of the world, his powers of contemplation, or his ability with language, but on the volume and omnipresence of his narrating voice" (240). Thus the reason the megaphone guy is listened to is because he is the only guy talking and he is loud. This extended metaphor becomes more obviously connected to the media as he goes on. Then the last line of the story, made into its own paragraph for greater impact, explains what the megaphone guy has actually done to the partygoers: "He has, in effect, put an intelligence-ceiling on the party" (Saunders 240). This format of story building allows Saunders to criticize and exemplify a real life situation without pointing fingers and while capturing the reader's attention. This also allows the reader to look at the situation from a different perspective and to start thinking critically about what is being said and how it relates to aspects of the reader's own life. Saunders uses casual storytelling throughout the essay to promote certain ideas and offer concrete examples of situations that he believes are occurring. Through these strategies, he hopes to sway readers to his point of view.

In addition to using hypothetical examples, Saunders uses easily identifiable real life references such as the O.J. Simpson trial: "Because the premise of the crime's national importance was obviously false, it had to be bolstered. […] To wring thousands of hours of coverage from what could have been summarized in a couple of minutes every few weeks, a new rhetorical strategy was developed, or—let's be generous—evolved" (241). By using a recognizable reference, he gives his audience a real life example of something they themselves most likely saw and remember. Saunders can also break down a real world example and explain what the media is doing with it. By using these real life references, he supports his case; he makes those hypothetical situations a plausible exaggeration of situations that actually happened that a reader can either remember or look up. By telling the hypothetical stories first, Saunders makes himself more interesting to listen to and more captivating.

7. There is something about the way writing is spaced that fools our brains into thinking it is doing more or less work when it isn't. How many times have you exhaled a sigh of relief when a teacher says she wants a paper double- rather than single-spaced? How many times has a teacher asked for a paper to be double-spaced?

Students like the double-spacing because they seem to think it means less work, and teachers like it because they get lots of white space while they read twenty-five similar essays. When we read, our brains like organization and blank space. Organizing an essay in a way that fools the reader into thinking they are not reading as much as they are is a good way to keep someone reading an essay because they do it without even realizing it.

Another neat idea to format an essay is to use number breaks or headlines because you can jump from idea to idea without confusing your reader. Take the way I bounce between these little anecdotes and talking about Saunders' essay, for example.

8. Another aspect of Saunders' writing that lends strength to his storytelling is the way he formats the essay. He separates the essay into numbered, chapter-like chunks. This strategy makes the essay easier to read, allowing the brain to read a portion and then pause before reading the next portion. This also lends to his storytelling, allowing him to write a new story from scratch in each segment and then relate it to ideas or real world events. It also allows for quick changes of subject so that he can mention something and then quickly move on to something else. Remind you of anything? Saunders' breaks from one story (and topic) to another unfold in the same way as TV news. His form echoes his content. But Saunders also introduces responsible

and thought-provoking ideas through his stories, getting the reader to think and question, unlike the news media he is criticizing. Also, by giving the reader small pieces of an idea and then creating a break before moving onto the next idea, Saunders allows his audience to mentally process what he has said so that they can begin to think critically. Thus, since his primary objective is to get the reader to question his or her relationship with the news media, it works in his favor to have separate chapters in his essay.

9. All the aspects of Saunders' essay are designed to have the reader question things that they take for granted and might never have questioned before. He also designs the essay to make his ideas accessible and understandable to a wide audience. Through his voice, persona, format, and clever storytelling, Saunders makes himself intriguing to more readers. By reaching a broader group of readers, he may more readily help people question how the news media manipulates us and what the news media deems important so we will begin trying to change its negative impact on society.

10. By mimicking Saunders' rhetoric in this essay, I hope I have made you think about how the way information is presented to you makes a difference in how you receive it. The effectiveness of style, format, and language all influence how we perceive what is being said to us. They also affect how and if we interact with a text, whether we like it, hate it, believe it, or stop reading it altogether. Saunders' rhetorical choices were effective and thought provoking as, I hope, you have also found them here.

Work Cited

Saunders, George. "The Braindead Megaphone." *Other Words: A Writer's Reader*. Eds. David Fleming et al. Dubuque: Kendall Hunt, 2009. 239–248. Print.

Adding to the Conversation

Preface

For the unit called "Adding to the Conversation," each student travels even further into a wider public audience by taking part in a larger conversation around a subject or issue that s/he finds meaningful. What appeals to each student, what they find important and meaningful, has so much to do with their own histories and experiences. Students begin with a question, research multiple perspectives on the larger conversation around their question, and then imagine a potential audience that ought to hear more about it. Finding a point of entry where they can contribute meaningfully to this dialogue, students then write essays for a specific and more public audience—essays that include representation of and responses to sources but that are ultimately guided by the student's purpose. Here are essays that move beyond the "academic" world.

These essays are evidence of how writing serves the community. In the following essays, the writers bring their perspectives into the "world" and make their voices integral to larger conversations.

Shoeless and Shameless

JUSTIN CALDERARA

Justin Calderara explores the conversation within the running community around the merits of unshod running in order to inform readers about the benefits and drawbacks of the technique. He draws upon various resources, including personal observation, interviews, biographies, and scholarly articles, to present a balanced perspective of his topic. Calderara's repetition of the first person calls attention to both his place within a community and the narrative of his research process, which is as important as the research itself.

The community of runners from across the world is undergoing a drastic change. At first what I saw was hard to believe, but then I continued to see it. It started to seem like I couldn't go one day without watching a shoeless runner go by. You may have seen these barefoot runners for yourself; running unshod has become a popular trend with runners over recent years, to which my first question was—why? It seems strange that the impressive advancements in athletic footwear have not convinced people that running shod is the way to run. Who could resist sporting Nike's newest shoe on a leisurely run through the park? Apparently, an entire legion of people has resisted the urge, and this trend does not seem to be slowing. The more I see barefoot runners, the more I question my shod running style. Is running barefoot actually better, or is the new hype all over nothing? I wanted answers to my questions, so I began my investigation of runners and historical trends in order to see exactly what has inspired runners to lose their shoes.

To begin my search, I first focused on my prior knowledge of barefoot running. Everything I knew before this investigation came from simple observations during high school track workouts. I tried many different running styles as a track athlete, one of which was barefoot running. I once experimented with this technique on a treadmill and noticed that I tended to land on the balls of my feet more often when running unshod—a trend that supposedly encourages more natural strides and foot strikes. This stride was uncomfortable and foreign at first, yet I imagine I could have grown to like it given proper time. The difference was clear when I laced my shoes back up and began running again. I could feel my heels falling heavily to the ground, which seemed awkward and painful after running so lightly. After my run, I was able to watch some friends complete the same exercise. It was easy to see that the weight of the shoe affected their strides, and their feet clearly landed more gently when unshod. I was only able to make broad observations, which left me wanting to know more. This workout made me curious and inspired me to ask more experienced barefoot runners about their style.

I decided to call my former cross-country coach, Robert Bouchard. Bouchard has competed unshod in several marathons and triathlons over his lifetime. In our interview, Bouchard described his transition from shod to barefoot running as "one of the best decisions I have ever made." Though it took about two years for him to get used to, this change has allowed Bouchard to move faster and more naturally. Additionally, he feels that this change has saved his legs from injuries he faced while running shod. He specifically noted that he "enjoys the lightweight feeling of barefoot running" that has given him superior foot speed for a middle-aged man. I recall practices where Bouchard would soar past my teammates and me at the end of races because of his enhanced foot speed. Our conversation seems to suggest that running barefoot—after becoming comfortable with it—is a faster alternative to shod running. To see if others felt the same way, I continued my interviews.

UMass's campus was the next place I searched for interview participants. On such a large campus, it's difficult not to see at least one runner while walking around; interviewing these runners seemed like the perfect opportunity to receive feedback. When asked about his style of running, Robert Flanagan, a UMass freshman, said, "My parents urged me to try barefoot running since they had positive experiences with it. After two weeks, I still hadn't gotten used to it, so I quit." Unlike Bouchard, transitioning to barefoot running was too uncomfortable and painful for Flanagan to cope with. This was a common trend among the other runners I interviewed. Many runners said that they had tried or at least heard of barefoot running, but they were unable to adjust to it after running shod for so long. These results highlight the transition period from shod to unshod running as the main deterrent, which made me eager to find a college runner who had successfully made the change.

After some searching, I found some seasoned barefoot runners around campus. Brian Jin, a UMass freshman, raised a particularly interesting point, claiming "people ran barefoot for thousands of years before shoes were invented, and they were able to get by." Jin argues that it's more natural for people to run barefoot because that's what had been done until recently in our history. Furthermore, he sees no need to wear fancy new athletic shoes because he doesn't think they make runners faster or healthier. Seeing the human race as a historically barefoot population almost makes running barefoot seem normal. After hearing this, I followed Jin's thought and focused my research on the origins of barefoot running.

Runners have trained and competed barefoot for almost the entire existence of the human race. According to the article "Variation in Foot Strike Patterns during Running among Habitually Barefoot Populations," it was not until the mid-1800s that runners began wearing shoes. Several communities in Africa still run barefoot, including the Daasanach of northern Kenya who are studied in the article. Unlike the previous examples, these habitually barefoot people have run unshod for their entire history (Hatala et al. 1). Many scientists have concluded that people who run barefoot, such as the Daasanach, are at a lesser risk of ankle and heel injuries due to the nature of their stride. "Barefoot runners more often strike the ground with their midfoot," the article says, while "shod runners tend to land on their heels" (Hatala et al. 2).

Since the cushion in shoes is concentrated towards the back, shod runners feel safe landing on their heels because most of the impact is absorbed. However, this stride makes runners more susceptible to injury (Hatala et al. 2). When compared to other habitually barefoot populations, the Daasanach share similar patterns in foot strike and anatomy (Hatala et al. 2). These similarities suggest that shoes encourage runners to step differently than what is natural for the body. I was interested in exploring this thought more thoroughly and decided the best way to do so was to study a runner who excelled with both styles.

Amidst my search for such athletes, I discovered perhaps the greatest one: Abebe Bikila of Ethiopia, whom I read about in Paul Rambali's book, *Barefoot Runner: The Life of Marathon Champion Abebe Bikila*. Bikila was born into poverty in a small Ethiopian town, training hard every day to become a great runner. Though his people were not habitually barefoot, Bikila learned to run barefoot because his family could not afford shoes. He had become so accustomed to this that by the time the 1960 Olympic Marathon came about, Bikila decided to run barefoot just as he had practiced (Rambali 20). He won the marathon and became the first of several iconic barefoot Olympians from Africa in the modern era. Bikila went on to win the marathon in the following Olympics, this time shod. Yet, he continued to train barefoot following his monumental shod victory, stating that it was the natural way for him (Rambali 150). Though neither was necessarily faster or slower for him, Bikila chose to run barefoot for the remainder of his career because it was most natural to him. This example suggests that the choice between shod and barefoot is often about comfort rather than speed.

Studying Bikila showed me that I had not yet discussed how shod or unshod running affects race performance, which I assumed would determine many people's opinions on the two styles. There had clearly been great shod and barefoot runners, but I was still unable to compare the two without scientific evidence. Thus, my next point of research was to learn how the two styles affect speed and efficiency, two things racers need. One claim made in the article "Barefoot-Shod Running Differences: Shoe or Mass Effect?" was that "barefoot running was reported to be more efficient locomotion […] than shoe running" (Divert et al. 517). Shoes add weight to the feet, making runners slower and tiring them more quickly. The article continues to express how running shod requires a higher oxygen intake for the runner, making them more susceptible to exhaustion (Divert 517). A low breath rate is key to a runner's performance, which shod running is proven to increase. I found several sources mentioning similar detriments associated with shod running performance.

Another article, "What We Can Learn About Running From Barefoot Running: An Evolutionary Perspective," by Daniel Lieberman, shows that barefoot runners run with a higher stride frequency and longer strides than shod runners, allowing them to cover greater distance at a faster pace (69). Still, most elite competitive runners choose to run with shoes because "they protect the foot and allow one to run on rough surfaces without worrying about foot placement" (Lieberman 68). Runners who have not run barefoot for very long are more susceptible to wounds from landing on sharp rocks, yet the skin on the foot becomes tougher with more exposure. As much of my research shows, running barefoot becomes easier on the body after the initial transition period. Aside from this, barefoot running is painted in a positive light in these articles, which could leave the audience wondering—why do people ever run shod?

I, too, was asking this question after my research thus far. However, as I refined my research, I began finding articles mentioning the barefoot running myth. One such belief is that running unshod makes runners immune to injuries. According to Gretchen Reynolds' article, "Barefoot Running Can Cause Injuries, Too," "some people who take up barefoot running develop entirely new aches and injuries." The article discusses a study done in Utah between a group of shod runners and a group of first-time barefoot runners. After just ten weeks of daily five-mile runs, the beginnings of bone injuries were apparent in many of the unshod runner's feet. More importantly, the shod running group showed no injuries to the bones. Some runners even developed stress fractures in their heels during this time. From this data, sports doctors warned runners to be cautious when transitioning to barefoot running, perhaps running as little as one mile for the first few weeks (Reynolds).

As shown throughout my paper, the transition period is what deters most runners from ultimately becoming faithful barefoot runners. Without proper instruction, abandoning athletic footwear can be a painful and difficult task that often causes serious injuries to the legs and feet.

Luckily, there are experts who have perfected the art of barefoot running and happily share their secrets with the entire running community. Ken Bob Saxton, a dedicated barefoot runner, has devoted much of his life to aiding runners through the treacherous transition period. In his book, *Barefoot Running: Step by Step*, Saxton tells runners his secrets to running barefoot comfortably. As a shod runner, he experienced "drudgery, pain, and injury," which was later replaced by "fun, excitement, and speed" once he made his ten year long transition (Saxton 37). Saxton describes feeling restricted by his shoes, which he felt only slowed him down. Without shoes, he was able to soar through marathons at faster speeds and with less foot pain. In his tutorial book, he emphasizes patience when first starting, as it took him nearly ten years to feel comfortable running barefoot. He explains that with time, one's stride will correct itself and running without shoes will feel normal and enjoyable (Saxton 121). By being patient, Saxton argues that one will come to understand their natural stride and that shoes will only try to change it. As with many barefoot runners, Saxton's perseverance and passion for running propelled him through the transition process and provided yet another perspective for our debate.

In Saxton's piece he mentions other barefoot runners from throughout history who inspired him. Seeing this as an interesting chance to see how techniques have developed, I pursued this thought and found W.G. George. In the early 1900s, George was famous for creating a workout that shod and unshod runners found helpful for perfecting their strides called the "100-Up." This workout is referenced in Christopher McDougall's article, "The Once and Future Way to Run," where McDougall describes his and others' experiences with the exercise. The workout consists of three parts: springing from the toe, bringing the knee to the level of the hip, and repeating while alternating legs (McDougall). However simple, McDougall reveals that storied athletes such as Alberto Salazar and Mark Cucuzzella have said that the workout truly perfects one's stride, shod or unshod.

Until now, I had seen the two styles as separate with no common ground. Yet, it seems clear from this that regardless of style, one can run well and quickly if good form and habits are practiced regularly. After reading this article, I felt I had an answer to my question—which form of running is better?

In the concluding lines of her article "Is Barefoot Running Really Better?" Maggie Young states, "there is no perfect option" when deciding between running styles. Young continues on to say that while there are advantages and disadvantages to both shod and barefoot running, there is not a correct way to run as people may think. My findings have proven that there are fans of barefoot running just as there are those who find it uncomfortable. Regardless of personal opinion, both are just as good, or bad, as the other. I found it impossible to draw one accurate conclusion when there are so many varying preferences, all of which suit the individual runner perfectly. I may look strangely at barefoot runners when I see them out on the road, but I'm wrong to say these people are running improperly or that my form of running is superior.

As far as injuries, studies clearly show that any form of running will cause injuries—shod or unshod. Young is correct in stating that there is no right answer to this question, and no scientific evidence can change your personal preference. My second-guessing is done; I now feel confident with my running style because it works for me. Don't focus on which form is better; focus on which form is better for you. If this means making the leap from shod to barefoot or vice versa, so be it. What I mean to stress is that the transition from one to the other should be gradual, calculated, and honest. Don't change your style because you want to follow popular trends; rather, change your style because it feels right to you.

Works Cited

Bouchard, Robert. Telephone Interview. 2 Apr. 2013.

Divert, C., et al. "Barefoot-Shod Running Differences: Shoe or Mass Effect?" *International Journal of Sports Medicine* 29.6 (2008): 512–18. Print.

Flanagan, Robert. Personal Interview. 6 Apr. 2013.

Hatala, Kevin G., et al. "Variation in Foot Strike Patterns during Running among Habitually Barefoot Populations." *PLOS One* 8.1 (2013): 1–6. Web. 1 Apr. 2013.

Jin, Brian. Personal Interview. 6 Apr. 2013.

Lieberman, Daniel E. "What Can We Learn about Running from Barefoot Running: An Evolutionary Medical Perspective." *Exercise and Sports Science Review* 40.2 (2012): 63–72. Print.

McDougall, Christopher. "The Once and Future Way to Run." *New York Times.* New York Times, 2 Nov. 2011. Web. 18 Apr. 2013.

Rambali, Paul. *Barefoot Runner: The Life of Marathon Champion Abebe Bikila.* London: Serpent's Tail Limited, 2006. Print.

Reynolds, Gretchen. "Barefoot Running Can Cause Injuries, Too." *New York Times.* New York Times, 6 Mar. 2013. Web. 2 Apr. 2013.

Saxton, Ken B., and Roy M. Wallack. *Barefoot Running Step by Step: Barefoot Ken Bob, the Guru of Shoeless Running, Shares His Personal Technique for Running with More Speed, Less Impact, Fewer Leg Injuries, and More Fun.* Beverly, MA: Fair Winds Press, 2011.

Young, Maggie. "Is Barefoot Running Really Better?" Web log post. *Men's Fitness.* Men's Fitness. 26 Mar. 2013. Web. 6 Apr. 2013.

The Influence of the Disney Princess on the Evolution of Women

NOEL CASEY

The terms first-, second-, and third-wave do not just apply to the feminist movement: as Noel Casey points out, they can also parallel the progression of Disney princesses in the twentieth century. Casey reflects upon her personal experience of growing up with the various versions of Disney's princesses as she evaluates the critical conversation surrounding them. Her use and integration of quotes, as well as her attention to nuance, speaks to the lasting place that Disney princesses have in our culture, for better or for worse.

Stories and their characters often have the ability to hold a presence in our lives, throughout our childhood and well into adulthood. A character that has been a constant influence on the values, ideals, and aspirations of young girls and women since the early 20th century is the image of the Disney princess. Many young girls, including me, have grown up watching these movies and emulating these characters for many different reasons. However, the Disney princess has been criticized by some as "anti-feminist" because of her dependence on a "prince" to rescue and take care of her. Critics have also complained about her exaggerated traditional feminine traits such as cleaning or singing. But others have praised Disney's portrayal of these young girls' coming-of-age tales where they discover what they want out of life and expect for themselves. As time has progressed, not only have women been making strides in society; so has the image of the Disney princess. She continues to influence women with her spunk, ambition, and big dreams by deviating from her original archetype to represent more modern ideals and values of women today while still being able to find her "happily ever after." I believe that Disney princesses are a positive influence on young girls and should not be criticized for how they portray women. Rather, they should be praised for how they have evolved along with real women and maintained their status as important media characters while incorporating modern day values into their stories and characters.

The princess has long been an icon transcending time. In her essay "The Princess and the Magic Kingdom: Beyond Nostalgia, the Function of the Disney Princess," author Rebecca Rozario states that "the princess is a fairy-tale staple and even in the world's republic, she continues to be re-drawn. She has remained a relevant anachronism over centuries, through revolutions, wars, and globalization" (34). While the image of a princess has changed throughout history, she has remained a constant figure for young girls to emulate as an unofficial guide into womanhood. Specifically, the Disney princess has been called "the princess of all princesses" (Rozario 34), thus reigning supreme in young girls' lives and memories. When I was growing up, I would watch Disney's princess movies repeatedly, dress up as my favorites, and dream of the day I'd marry my prince. My favorites ranged from the classics to the new modern releases. I emulated these princesses for different reasons, some superficial, some not. As a little girl, I was entranced by the glamor of their lives: the ball gowns, horse-drawn carriages, castles, and magic, but as I grew older I respected the courage, determination, compassion, and loyalty along with many other values these women possessed. I think that these characteristics are important to teach young women, and I believe these traits have had a positive influence on my life. The world around us is constantly changing and progressing, but these princesses still continue to influence me as well as other young girls and women. Each time I watch one of these movies, I find something new to relate to and realize how powerful the message of the female identity is, and has continued to be, for generations.

Disney's princesses are generally synonymous with society's image of women at that particular time. Critics have often disparaged Disney's early princesses for this reason: "some have sought to reveal her beauty as stereotype, her good nature as submissiveness" (Rozario 34). However, when *Snow White and the Seven Dwarfs* was first released in 1937, America was recovering from the Great Depression. At that time, most women were dependent on their husbands, not encouraged to work or attend school, and were seen primarily as caretakers for their children. This was society's idea and plan for women at that time. In her article, "The Princess Problem," Laura Vanderkam believes that this image was portrayed through Snow White and has aided in a lack of "internal locus of control" in girls. Vanderkam believes that girls were not being taught to be responsible for their own futures. She states, "'Prince Charming is going to save you.' Best to marry a high-earning man, because your husband will determine the standard of living for you and your children" (Vanderkam 9). This storyline is seen in Disney's three original princesses— Snow White, Cinderella, and Aurora who were all "rescued" from some form of peril or peasant life by their prince. In my opinion, Disney did not create this image of "helpless" women, but was simply responding to it by "linking 'princesshood' to contemporary concepts of ideal girlhood" (Whelan 25). These were not traits that Disney deemed as traditional or stereotypical; it was society's opinion of women that led to the stereotype portrayed in Disney movies. I am not trying to disregard the fact that today this is an outdated depiction of women, but the image of the princess presented in *Snow White and the Seven Dwarfs, Cinderella,* and *Sleeping Beauty* "continued to conform to societal convention regarding girls and their place in society" (Whelan 23). Despite these critics, Snow White, Cinderella, and Princess Aurora have remained icons in the eyes of little girls for over two centuries and continue to dictate certain feminine characteristics and aspirations.

As history has progressed, however, women have become more respected; their role in society has become more important and appreciated. Women aren't just considered caretakers but are given higher positions in the workplace, are attending school longer, and are becoming more independent overall. It has also become more acceptable for women to steer away from the "traditional" path of getting married and having children. Many women do not feel the same pressure to follow this path and often wait until later in life or decide to deviate completely from this ideal. This evolution of women has not gone unnoticed by Disney who has adapted its product to reflect this change. *The Little Mermaid, Beauty and the Beast, Mulan, Aladdin,* and *Pocahontas* were all released at the end of the 20th century, over 70 years after Walt Disney first released *Snow White and the Seven Dwarfs.* These "second wave princesses," as they are commonly referred to, deviate from their stereotypical princess predecessors. Ariel, Belle, Mulan, Princess Jasmine, and Pocahontas aren't "typical" princesses who are ultra-feminine or dependent on men. In fact, these women are against loveless marriages and don't rely on men to rescue them from their troubles. Instead of succumbing to the traditional ideals of their fathers and society, each one sets off on her own journey of self-discovery. Their spunkiness, big dreams, and refusal to conform to society's traditions make them the antithesis of Disney's earlier princesses and more relatable to modern day young girls and women.

The second wave princesses are often referred to as "heroines" because of their departure from the image society had of the princess based on Disney's earlier adaptations. Ariel is "motivated by the desire to explore the human world and willing to take a risk in defining the subject and object of her desires" (Whelan 26), and Princess Jasmine's "greatest desire is to experience life outside the palace as an ordinary person" (Whelan 26). Belle, "a book-loving young woman who refused the attentions of the town 'hunk' in favor of continuing her reading habits" (Whelan 25), and finding "adventure in the great wide somewhere" is also an example of a princess with more modern-day values. These girls aren't dreaming of when their prince will come to rescue them but dreaming of adventure, discovering and experiencing new things, and finding what they truly want out of life. Two more princesses that defy the stereotype put forth by Disney's original princesses are Mulan and Pocahontas who are far from similar to Cinderella, Snow White, and Princess Aurora. They are both warriors engaging in battle, and "heroism, egalitarianism, and autonomy are slipped into the conventions of Disney princesshood" (Rozario 47) as they stray from their families and specifically avoid their fathers' aspirations of marriage for them. Despite these more modern values, many feminists still criticize these second wave princesses as having anti-feminist attributes. Although these princesses have aspirations and moments of independence, ultimately they do all fall in love and end up sacrificing their freedom, family, or even their own voice for a man. Bridget Whelan, author of "Power to the Princess: Disney and the Creation of the 20th Century Princess Narrative," believes this image negatively affects young girls who are then, "strongly positioned to believe, in the end, that desire, choice, and empowerment are closely linked to catching and loving a handsome man" (Whelan 26).

However, I think that the way these girls pursue their true love isn't anti-feminist and has still evolved from Disney's early images. The second wave princesses don't necessarily go looking for love, but fall into it. With their love comes sacrifice, but in reality most relationships require sacrifices from both partners. These women realize that they can find love without compromising their dreams. In her article, "What's wrong with Cinderella?" Peggy Orenstein considers that "maybe princesses are in fact a sign of progress, an indication that girls can embrace their predilection for pink without compromising strength or ambition; that, at long last, they can 'have it all'" (Orenstein). I believe that this image of the princess is a much more powerful, realistic, and relatable way to highlight the modern day girl's values. She should be encouraged to follow her dreams and be different, but she also shouldn't be criticized for wanting companionship and love from a young prince, who in turn will sacrifice and fight for her the same way she has for him.

Now, well into the 21st century, Disney has continued to adapt their princesses to identify with modern women. Three of Disney's newest projects, *The Princess and the Frog, Brave,* and *Frozen* are praised for their portrayal of princesses who are even more independent and relatable than even the second wave of princesses. I believe that women today are influenced by the princess images of the past but not defined by them. Women have constantly been evolving and will continue to because of the strife that has plagued us for centuries. As women we are taught to be many things: compassionate yet stern; independent yet loyal; feminine yet not submissive. The dichotomy of women is often hard to understand and accept, yet Disney movies help women put these characteristics into perspective and help us identify who we want to be and what we want out of life. I believe that you can have attributes of the princess and the heroine as well as maintain your individuality. I think Disney gives the princess attributes of real women because that is who their characters are modeled after, taking the best traits of women and exaggerating those to cinematic proportions to prove that it's possible for women to harmonize the two aspects of their roles in society and truly live "happily ever after."

Works Cited

Do Rozario, Rebecca-Anne. "The Princess and the Magic Kingdom: Beyond Nostalgia, the Function of the Disney Princess." *Women's Studies in Communication* 27.1 (2004). Print.

Orenstein, Peggy. "What's wrong with Cinderella?" *New York Times Magazine*. New York Times 24 Dec. 2006: 34–39. Web. 2 Apr. 2014.

Vanderkam, Laura. "The Princess Problem." *USA Today* 12 Aug. 2009. Web. 2 Apr. 2014.

Whelan, Bridget. "Power to the Princess: Disney and the Creation of the 20th Century Princess Narrative." *Interdisciplinary Humanities* 29.1 (2012): 21–34. Web. 1 Apr. 2014.

Silent Spectator Seeking Solutions in the South Shore

DANIELLE FAHEY

From the beginning, Danielle Fahey's personal anecdote about watching friends smoke high doses of Oxycodone grabs you and refuses to let go. Her essay incorporates personal interviews, news articles, and drug statistics in order to understand the rise in drug abuse on the South Shore. Fahey ends with a deeper understanding of the issue than when she began, and leaves her readers with the responsibility of not remaining silent witnesses to this growing abuse.

As I sat on a friend's couch watching *Family Guy*, I could hear the boys whispering behind me. They were being strange—sketchy even—so I turned around and looked over at them; the conversation stopped. As I asked, "What are you guys talking about?" Pat* walked over and sat beside me. "Fahey," he started, "I know I can trust you, and you're the shit and one of the coolest people I know, so please don't freak out or anything, but we're about to smoke some jams." I froze. They were smoking Percocet 30s, prescription pain relievers similar to Oxycodone. "Why?" I inquired. "I don't know," he chuckled, "because we want to. Don't worry. It's not a big deal. You're cool. Don't say anything to anyone, though." The boys came and sat down around me and began folding up squares of tinfoil and crushing the small blue pills onto them. As they began lighting the bottoms of the foil, a scent of marshmallow filled the air. I scrolled through my phone trying to distract my eyes from the scene unfolding in front of me, but it was odd, the whole situation—I was sitting in a room with a group of close friends as they smoked prescription pills to get high. Essentially, I was watching them begin to throw their lives and futures away, but I was silent. Maybe it was because the smell wasn't worrisome, or maybe because they weren't using needles and spoons, or maybe I was just too scared to say something, but I sat there quietly and patiently, waiting for them to finish and continue on with the night.

"All right, let's play X-Box," muttered Pat. I was relieved that it was over and that things could go back to normal. But when I looked around the room

---

* Names have been changed to protect the identities of participants

and saw their eyes glazed over and their bodies lying lifelessly on the chairs, I realized it wasn't. I stayed for a half-hour longer in that little room, the only sound coming from the NHL game and a couple of mumbled conversations. I saw John passed out, sitting up in his seat, and it looked like the other three were about to do the same. As I shut the door and said bye, no one replied. There were no hugs, no "daps," no goodnights—only four bodies, motionless and mute, high off the drug.

Well-kept lawns, ranch-style houses, and dirt roads that lead to a lake don't exactly scream "Drug Abuse Danger Zone!" But despite the deceiving looks of innocence and unobtrusiveness, the small towns of south shore Massachusetts have been hotbeds for prescription pill and heroin abuse for the past few years. It's difficult to believe these "bedroom communities once considered immune to such problems" (Schiavone) have been the locations for over one hundred opiate related deaths in just a few years. "In 2009 and 2010, 31 men and women died of an overdose in those 10 towns [Abington, Hull, Cohasset, Hanover, Hingham, Marshfield, Pembroke, Scituate, Norwell, and Rockland]. That is one person every 23 days" (Schiavone). In addition, the neighboring towns of Weymouth, Quincy, and Braintree had 91 deaths in that same two-year period; that is one death every 8 days (Schiavone). Things have only worsened since 2010, and I haven't seen signs of it slowing down. It's possible that at fifteen, I wasn't old enough to know abusers, but it's also possible that the regularity of knowing an addict has increased. These numbers are alarming, but the stories and struggles of each number, each person, are what is even sadder and more difficult to understand.

In a study conducted by Alfred Lindesmith, it was found that many abusers began using heroin when in a group of already abusing peers (qtd. in Inciardi 99). I found this to be true when interviewing a friend, Nick Gormley, about his heroin addiction:

> I did it basically because the kids I started hanging out with (class of 2011) were doing them [prescription pills] at the time…and that's generally how everyone starts. They're hanging out with people who are doing them and think they are bigger and stronger than the drug and think they can do it for fun here and there and not get addicted.

It's scary to think about this in relation to the epidemic on the south shore, where illicit drug abuse in the past month, as well as the rate of drug induced deaths and treatment admission exceeds the national average (U.S. National Office of Drug Control). With the drugs so easily accessible and with so many users, it's worrisome that the chances of being put into a situation like Gormley describes, or having someone you know put in such a situation, are very real, and frankly, quite likely. I am a talented athlete, successful student, and a hard worker—I am far from the stereotypical image of someone who is surrounded by drugs. But many abusers are far from the image too; my friends didn't look like the kinds of kids who would snort dope, but it turned out that they were. In an article posted by the *Patriot Ledger*, the backgrounds of five local overdoses are described: "One was a 24-year-old nursing student from Hull. Others were a 41-year-old carpenter from Hingham, a 41-year-old fisherman from Scituate, a 49-year-old real estate developer from Hanover, an 18-year-old student from Norwell" (Schiavone). Heroin "does not discriminate on the basis of age, sex or lot in life" (Encarnacao).

It seems that addiction is something that happens subconsciously, often without warning or much notice. Users start off trying the drug "just once" but suddenly they are getting high daily. No one *thinks* that it's going to happen, and they certainly didn't plan on it. It is simply something that just *happens*. Inciardi bluntly states, "Users typically think that addiction will not happen to them" (99). But what happens when it does? One study found that addicts were more likely to abuse as they became stressed out or unhappy. Also, they found that when an addict heard, saw, or discussed the drug, their addiction was triggered (Preston and Epstein 29). As I interviewed a friend who has battled with his opiate addiction for some time now, I asked why he kept using the drug, even after reaching one of the lowest points of his life. Mike answered:

> I'd cry my eyes out randomly because of how badly I get depressed when I'm not using it. I was going strong [without heroin] when I saw a commercial about addiction, and it put getting high in my head. I thought, eh I'll only do it once, knowing damn well what would happen, and when I woke up after getting high, feeling not dope sick but disgusted with myself, I got high again to take away the pain, even though the better choice would be to accept the fact I messed up and move on.

"Why people use heroin, or any illicit drug for that matter, is not altogether understood" (Inciardi 99). In fact, it is something I do not understand at all.

As an onlooker and a friend, I have become increasingly concerned about the problem occurring right in my hometown. I know many users are tempted to try it because of the drug's sensations and the feeling of euphoria that they become addicted to, and I know peer pressure is an influence in testing it out. Once someone is addicted, I know there is not only a psychological addiction, but a physical one too. I know a battle with a heroin addiction is not an easy one, and I am thankful every day for my strong will to never sample it. But what I don't know is how can we prevent it?

I suppose if the answer to that question were so easy, there would be no such thing as addiction, and the psychologist who found the answer would be vacationing somewhere in Turks and Caicos. However, I feel there must be *something* we can do. Can we educate our peers on the dangers and effects of the drugs? Can we make an example of full-blown addicts and show how their lives have digressed? Can we realize that each person who has overdosed, each number in those statistics, is different and may need different treatments? Also, how can we prevent something that is so well disguised behind nice public schools and lovely cul-de-sacs? When I began writing this paper, I thought that I may have known a solution to the problem. However, through interviews and research, I have found that there is a lot more that goes into a heroin addiction than just weak willpower and a needle. In fact, I may have only found that there may never be an exact solution to something so complex and unruly.

I have learned one thing though: if you are sitting in a room where you know something bad is about to unfold, do not divert your eyes, do not silence your voice. Simply use reverse peer pressure, calmly and kindly, and remind those around you of what they are about to do to their lives and the lives of their friends and families; you may save their lives, or at least not let these drugs claim another victim. At the end of our interview, Mike told me, "I feel like a prisoner to this shit," and that is not a way you want a friend to feel.

Works Cited

Encarnacao, Jack. "Death Certificates Tell Story of Complex South Shore Overdose Epidemic." *Patriot Ledger*. Patriot Ledger, 20 Feb. 2012. Web. 6 Nov. 2013.

Gormley, Nick. Message to Danielle Fahey's iPhone. 5 Nov. 2013. Text Message.

Inciardi, James A. *The War on Drugs IV: The Continuing Saga of the Mysteries and Miseries of Intoxication, Addiction, Crime, and Public Policy*. Boston, MA: Pearson/Allyn and Bacon, 2008. 89–113. Print.

Nelson, Mike. Message to Danielle Fahey's iPhone. 5 Nov. 2013. Text Message.

Preston, Kenzie, and David Epstein. "Stress in the Daily Lives of Cocaine and Heroin Users: Relationship to Mood, Craving, Relapse Triggers, and Cocaine Use." *Psychopharmacology* 218.1 (2011): 29–37. *Academic Search Premier*. Web. 6 Nov. 2013.

Schiavone, Christian. "Small Towns on South Shore Not Immune to Drug Deaths." *Patriot Ledger*. Patriot Ledger, 25 June 2012. Web. 31 Oct. 2013.

United States Office of National Drug Control Policy. *Massachusetts Drug Control Update*. US Office of National Drug Control Policy, n.d. Web. 6 Nov. 2013.

Regarding the Truth of Legends

AMANDA KEOHANE

Drawing upon historical documents and literary criticism, Amanda Keohane uses a hometown legend of Lucy Keyes's disappearance in the eighteenth century as an emblem for probing the place and role of legends in our cultural imagination. Keohane enters this conversation through a personal anecdote and calls our attention to the importance of context and discourse in shaping our conceptions of "truth" across time.

I rolled the feather back and forth between my forefinger and my thumb, feeling the smooth and cool stem under my unmarred skin. I breathed deeply, picking up hints of the soil on which it had once laid and the scent of the autumn leaves that had scattered the cemetery. It filled me with a sense of calm and understanding, but at the same time I now saw everything differently, all thanks to the field trip we had been taken on. It was *the* field trip, the one that introduced us to our town's history and the legends people tell of it.

We hear all the time of legends, myths, and other such categories of storytelling, but what exactly *is* a legend? Amy Lowell, a Pulitzer Prize winning poet from the 1920s, describes a legend as "something which nobody has written and everybody has written, and which anybody is at liberty to rewrite. It may be altered, it may be viewed from any angle, it may assume what dress the author pleases, yet it remains essentially the same" (v). Legends do not begin like fables or fairy tales; they are not written and *then* spread by word—they begin by word of mouth and are *then* written down, at which point the original story has most likely altered significantly. However, Jan Harold Brunvand, a professor with a PhD in Folklore, defines legends as "a number of unverified reports (that is, rumors)" (9). By comparing this scholarly take on the subject to the non-scholarly view of Amy Lowell, it would seem that most legends may be more accurately defined by combining the two propositions. Not only does a legend begin as an unverified report, as Brunvand suggests, but it is also a story which anyone can alter in order to fit his or her discourse more appropriately.

We stepped off the bus at noon and were herded like cattle down to the cemetery. Soon I began to feel the firm cement of the road beneath my feet crumble away and transform into an uneven dirt path, as though we were traveling back in time. Our guide brought us to the back of the cemetery to a large grave that read *In Memory of Martha Keyes*. There it was, so close I could touch it. The guide called us to attention and slowly began his story:

Lucy Keyes was only four years old when she disappeared over 250 years ago. It was rumored that she ventured into the woods alongside Wachusett Mountain in hopes of catching up to her sisters who had gone to fetch sand for the fire. Lucy's two sisters returned in haste but with no sign of Lucy. Martha, the girls' mother, asked where Lucy was, but the girls had never run into her. Martha, realizing that her daughter must have gotten lost in the woods, immediately set out in search of her. Martha searched until she was pushed to the edge of insanity, and she died never having found any evidence of where Lucy had gone or what had become of her.

Curious as to what I could find on the legend, I delved deeply into my town's history and discovered many things. First, in *The Vital Records of Princeton, Massachusetts*, I came across some rather intriguing information. Under "Births" I found a listing in the Keyes's section that read, "Lucretia, d. Robert and Martha, Sept 6, 1764" (43). I feel that Lucy could easily have been a nickname for Lucretia and therefore saw this as evidence that the legend might be true, though Jeremiah Hanaford's *History of Princeton, Massachusetts*, shows a flaw in this possibility. While the book mentions the disappearance of Lucy, in Hanaford's retelling, it was stated that the disappearance occurred on "the 14th of April, 1755" (17), nine years before her birth was even recorded in the vital records, making the legend impossible to have occurred at all.

Many years after the disappearance of little Lucy, a letter written by the Keyes's former neighbor, Tilley Littlejohn, was discovered. Within the letter, Littlejohn confessed to crossing paths with Lucy in the woods that day. He was drunk and in a rage for he and Robert Keyes—Lucy's father—had been quarrelling over property lines. In all his fury he ran after Lucy, threw her to the ground, and crushed her skull with a nearby rock. After realizing what he had done, he burned her body and buried it in a nearby crypt.

While the content of the letter seems to be the agreed resolution to the legend, there are still rumors that Lucy was kidnapped by passing Indians and taken north. Two men admitted to Robert Keyes that they had seen a white girl living among the Indians in Canada, knowing nothing of her origins except the phrase "Chuset Hill." We will never know what really happened to Lucy Keyes, but many say that on windy nights one can hear the sound of Martha searching for her long lost daughter, never resting until united once again with her little Lucy.

While this legend may have begun as fact, over the years it has become impossible to tell how much or in what ways it has changed. This, then, must beg the question: *how true are legends?* Truth in relation to story is a key element when considering legends. Lowell states that "if science be proven truth [...], legends might be described as speculative or apprehended truth" (vi) and that legends "are bits of fact, or guesses at fact, pressed into the form of a story"(v–vi). But Brunvand reminds us that "the truth never stands in the way of a good story" (6). No one wants to tell a boring story; therefore, if the truth isn't good enough, most would add embellishments so as to make it more engaging and impressive.

The truth of a story is also relative to our knowledge, defined by the different discourses which we take part in. In the essay "Telling Our Stories: Speaking Truth to Power," Sue Novinger and Catherine Compton-Lilly, professors focusing on literacy, suggest that "the stories we tell are shaped and constrained by the multiple and overlapping discourses that inhabit our lives" (195), and that "discourses shape ways of knowing, what can be known, what might count as reality, and what might count as 'truth'" (195). Turning back to Amy Lowell, who says that legends are "guesses at fact, pressed into the form of a story" (vi), we begin to understand that the truth of a story is dependent on the discourse through which we hear it. Lowell suggests that the truth is most likely not as true as the audience may have thought. Slowly, as these stories are filtered between discourses, the facts they may have contained may become less prominent as various informants alter the stories to fit the discourse they are a part of. For example, the two sources I observed with this legend, a historical discourse and a government record, provided two very opposing truths, but truth nonetheless. Perhaps our tour guide was giving another variant of the truth so that it would fit the present discourse.

I looked down at the base of the headstone and noticed a single, black feather. Quickly, when no one was looking, I bent down and took the feather from the grave and rolled it back and forth between my fingers. I still have that feather to this day. Whenever I see it I am once again reminded of that day in the graveyard and the story that I was told. Even to this day there are times when I still wonder: *Is it true?*

Works Cited

Blake, Francis E. *Vital Records of Princeton, Massachusetts, to the End of the Year 1849*. Worcester, Mass: F. P. Rice, 1902. Print.

Brunvand, Jan H., and Erik Brunvand. *The Truth Never Stands in the Way of a Good Story*. Urbana: University of Illinois, 2000. Print.

Hanaford, Jeremiah L. *History of Princeton, Worcester County, Massachusetts; Civil and Ecclesiastical; from Its First Settlement in 1739, to April 1852*. Worcester: C.B. Webb, Printer, 1852. Print.

Lowell, Amy. "Preface." *Legends*. Boston: Houghton Mifflin, 1921. v–xiv. Print.

Novinger, Sue, and Catherine Compton-Lilly. "Telling Our Stories: Speaking Truth to Power." *Language Arts* 83.3 (2005): 195–203. *JSTOR*. Web. 28 Oct. 2013.

Punchlines: A Defense of Controversial Comedy

ANTONIO VILLALOBOS-ORTIZ

Antonio Villalobos-Ortiz articulates and investigates the tension between stand-up comedians and the larger society they mock and satirize. Examining comedians Bill Hicks, Jon Stewart, and George Carlin, Villalobos-Ortiz hypothesizes the purposes of comedy—as conversation, as (dis)engagement, and finally, perhaps, as art. The scholarly articles and interviews he cites highlight the importance of cynicism and satire as controversial and necessary aspects of spurring cultural dialogue.

Comedy is a broad genus of entertainment. Its expanse covers everything from witty sketches and goofy slapstick, to dark stand-up routines. It's the latter that seems to draw the most negative attention. Sure, you may find Monty Python dull or the Three Stooges to be ridiculous, but most people would never join in a public outcry to see either of these apologized for. Stand-up is the subgenre of comedy that really seems to have monopolized the ability to rile up the masses, particularly for satirizing particular groups, institutions, or individuals. A quick Google search will list dozens of comedians who have been forced to apologize. Say you are at a stand-up show and hear a copious number of racial slurs coming from the stage. Or perhaps you are the victim of some form of abuse and hear a comedian making light of it. Would you be angry? Would you stand up and say something? It's understandable why some people might take issue with what appears to be trivializing racism and violence. It is not so rare for comedy to take the form of pointing out and poking fun, and often people take offense when they see themselves as being the butt of a joke. Comedy can very easily offend anybody it targets, and therefore there is a big push, especially among comedians, to dismiss their material. It is a way of absolving themselves, but is it fair?

It can be argued that there is utility in comedy to illuminate perspectives that may be dark, vulgar, politically incorrect. These perspectives may not be pleasant, but they allow for questioning the established order and confronting what is acceptable in today's world. Entities we live with every day such as government, business, and media can seem rather static, stuck in a purgatory of mediocrity and banality. It may seem crude and juvenile, but is there no utility in hearing Bill Hicks say, "F**k that? When did mediocrity and banality become a good image for your children?"(Hicks). When did our society, with all of its virtues and vices, become what we should aspire to be? A statement like this has a way of eliciting mixed feelings from audiences. You don't have to be hypersensitive to see that there is controversy embedded in these words. At the same time, you don't have to be a cynic to see that meaning resides amidst the controversy. Are the points brought forth by comedy worth the offense and anger they can provoke, and if so, how can these two be reconciled?

Before comedy can be taken seriously or just dismissed, it needs to be established whether or not there really can be any substance to it. Take, for example, *The Daily Show*. Over the past decade, *The Daily Show* has been broadcasting four nights a week for most weeks of the year. While not strictly stand-up comedy, the two are stylistically very similar. They both focus on pointing out problems with everything from the political system to the media that covers it. Aside from providing some laughs, does the show serve any other purpose? In an article by Robert Hariman, he claims that the show, in a way, serves as an outlet for political deliberation. Humor, while being the basis for the show, serves as a tool for engagement. The real purpose behind the show is that it "continually calls the audience to informed participation, civil speech, and rational argument on behalf of sound public policy" (Hariman 274). Similarly, in an article by Geoffrey Baym, he advances the idea that "at its core, *The Daily Show* advocates a conversational or deliberative theory of democracy—a notion that only open conversation can provide the legitimate foundation for governance" (272). Both of these articles point to conversation—the sharing of ideas, thoughts, and opinions—as not only important but critical keys to sound social policy and government. *The Daily Show* has very clear utility when put into this context. Serving as a facilitator of conversation is enormously beneficial to society. Any form of media that encourages the spread of ideas has the potential to educate the public, and an educated public is most certainly a boon to society.

Something as carefully crafted as *The Daily Show* may help to fill an important niche in our society, but even through all its nitpicking and poking fun, it doesn't have the same level of shock value that some stand-up comedy does. Does this idea of being a conduit of discussion still apply? Indeed it does, perhaps to a larger extent, as it makes us call into question things that run deeper than government—things that are more intertwined with humanity. In an interview with George Carlin, one of the most well-known and revolutionary comedians to date, Carlin says, "I've given up on the whole human species. I think a big, good-sized comet is exactly what this species needs .... It would be terrible, and it would be wonderful" (Cooper). That global extinction of humanity is in some way deserved is a fairly unnerving statement. It certainly can't get any more controversial than a statement such as Carlin's. It is well outside the norm to in any way condone extinction. Carlin, however, brings a different perspective to his cynicism by saying, "But, you know, life is dual. If you'll scratch a cynic, you'll find a disappointed idealist" (Cooper). From this statement, and by watching much of his comedy, it becomes clear that Carlin hopes for his comet not because of a long-standing and deep-seated hatred for humanity. Rather it comes from a sense of disappointment in the way we are. Humans have the potential to do so much good for one another, but we find ourselves toiling with wars, grasping for material possessions, transfixed by mindless entertainment, and what Hicks referred to above as worship of "banality and mediocrity." It is even possible to look at this situation beyond societal transgressions. Is it so hard to understand Carlin's extreme position when we look retrospectively at our own lives? All humans, to varying degrees, have some sort of regret. We are imperfect. We have all done things we're not proud of, made mistakes, sinned. Carlin's words aim to point out precisely that; they aim to point out our flaws so that we may see them and learn from them, so that we develop some sympathy and personal responsibility in an age where it is often lacking. We may not agree that mass extinction is deserved, but the idea that we as a species and as individuals are not living to our full potential is a reasonable opinion, and it is important to put that opinion on the table. It is crucial that we don't dismiss his ideas as the ravings of a cynic. We should instead look at them as the words of a "parodist, a satirist, a comic engaging in political humor in the manner of Aristophanes, Erasmus, Mark Twain, Will Rogers, Richard Pryor, Garry Trudeau, and many, many others"(Hariman 274). The goal of this kind of comedy is to function as satire, and satire is crucial to our society, no matter how distasteful it may be.

So much of what is wrong with our society today can be traced to the lack of communication and the lack of knowledge that is the result. It is this problem that makes the need for satire evident. Politicians and the people behind them, your "owners" as Carlin would put it, make false promises, assert lies, and generally don't see themselves as culpable. It is the duty of satire to combat this. In his article about the importance of satire, Peter Goodrich points out that "the satirical concern is with the over-statements, the false assertions, the follies and vices that come with the solemnized rites, the sacral assertions, and the obscure practices of legal actors"(51). Satire is an enormously powerful tool for facilitating conversation about topics that seem too high above the everyman. To the average person, something as big as government can seem so far above one's head and reach. Satire can point out the structural instabilities in the construct that is government or society. Its very purpose is to point out stupidity and vices. It has a way of leveling the playing field, putting a human face on what is ultimately a human institution. Anything with this amount of power should not be so readily dismissed. Furthermore, satire allows for introspection. By making it understandable that large institutions are run by people, it becomes possible for individuals to see that their personal shortcomings can affect the world around them. The knowledge that our actions are not performed in a vacuum, that they can have an impact on others, makes it important for us to address our own flaws. Satire is truly powerful in that it can help us to change both ourselves and the world we live in.

So how does one reconcile these two very distinct aspects of comedy? On one hand, we have the ability to offend and anger the population, and on the other, we have the ability to educate them. The way that they can be reconciled is by the acknowledgment that comedy is an art, and like any other art form, it should not only be taken seriously, but should also be analyzed to be fully understood. Like any other art form, it has the ability to captivate and move people. This does not mean, though, that we should take everything every comedian says literally. There are deeper meanings to any work of art, and comedy is no exception. In fact, comedy may be one of the most effective forms of satire, as "the virtue of humor is precisely its effectiveness, its ability to cut to the quick. Those who have nothing to hide have nothing to fear from laughter" (Goodrich 54).

Works Cited

Baym, Geoffrey. "The Daily Show: Discursive Integration and the Reinvention of Political Journalism." *Political Communication* 22.3 (2005): 259–276. *Taylor and Francis*. Web. 28 Oct. 2013.

Bill Hicks: Relentless. Dir. Chris Bould. Perf. Bill Hicks. 1992. Web. 28 Oct. 2013.

Cooper, Marc. "The Progressive Interview: George Carlin." *The Progressive* 07 (2001): 32–7. *Progressive.com*. 23 June 2008. Web. 27 Oct. 2013.

Goodrich, Peter. "The Importance of Being Earnest: Satire and the Criticism of Law." *Social Semiotics* 15.1 (2005): 43–58. *Academic Search Premier*. Web. 27 Oct. 2013.

Hariman, Robert. "In Defense of Jon Stewart." *Critical Studies in Media Communication* 24.3 (2007): 273–277. *Academic Search Premier*. Web. 27 Oct. 2013.

Writer's Statement

Preface

College Writing ends with a "Writer's Statement," where students review the portfolios they have written for the course and harvest some of the most important insights they have discovered—about writing and about themselves as writers. By analyzing their struggles, their choices, and their triumphs, they compare their past learning with their present knowledge in order to illuminate where they will need to go as writers in their futures. Learning to write well is a never-ending process, so this "Writer's Statement" is, in fact, a beginning that launches the student into the world of academic writing and beyond. Students consider the various "tools" they have assembled in their writer's "toolbox": revision, responding to writing, reflecting on writing, writing for an audience and context, writing with purposefulness and the consciousness of crafting an idea into extended prose.

These following texts are the result of each student's unique experience of *College Writing*. They range from larger insights about the self and about learning to wonderfully pragmatic advice for any writer. We hope you enjoy reading about these students' journeys through *College Writing*, and the wisdom they gleaned as they worked throughout the course. Their advice and the insights they share serve as inspiration for us all.

Written Fractals and Other Authorial Paradigms

RICHELLE COHEN

Covering one's history as a writer from kindergarten to College Writing *seems a Herculean task, but Richelle Cohen accomplishes this through narrating key experiences, selecting critical details, and exploring her personal context as a writer. Thus she implicitly explores how she met the goals of* College Writing *and explicitly expresses what she has learned about her writing process.*

With the pencil clenched between my three fingers, I drew a quick breath. Months of practice culminated in this point. I could either spell my name or I wouldn't be accepted into my first year of grammar school.

What seems now like a perfunctory task was originally the most difficult I had ever encountered. It wasn't that I didn't know how to write a name; I mastered those hand motions months—if not years—before: R-I-C-K-I. Somehow this told adults that my name was Ricki, though I didn't yet understand how. The trouble, however, was that I didn't know how to spell my real name: Richelle. My parents thought up my nickname before finding the real one. I was raised using the name Ricki; I didn't even react to the name Richelle. How was I supposed to know how to use letters I didn't understand to form a name I didn't respond to?

And yet, with the coaching of my parents during dinner—using the scientifically-proven doodling-in-mashed-potatoes method—and some residual confusion (during which I would introduce myself to others as "Rickirichellebeth Cohen"), I spelled my real name well enough to be admitted into kindergarten. My struggle with writing had begun.

After mastering the writing of my name, I learned about the intricacies of the paragraph. To do this, we used a color-based system. We placed sentences inside green rectangles if they were the introduction or conclusion, placed the main reasons inside pink rectangles, and placed the supporting details in yellow rectangles. Every sentence had its place; nothing could fit outside the context of those little rectangles. If it didn't fit within a rectangle, it didn't belong in the paragraph. That was the only way to write a proper paragraph.

With the paragraph under my belt, I could now learn how to tackle the five paragraph essay. I found the exercise daunting but realized that it didn't really differ from an extensive paragraph. You had to introduce your topic. After introductions, you listed the main arguments, supporting them this time with entire paragraphs instead of sentences. Simple enough.

Just after I thought I understood the mechanics of the essay, they challenged us with the research paper. Papers were a never-ending source of anxiety because I had to focus on supporting a meaningful and concise thesis while simultaneously expanding the thoughts to satisfy that word count. (Signing my name became the best part of writing an essay by absorbing two whole words from the word count.) Research papers were expansions on essays, which, in turn, were expansions on paragraphs, the inevitable outcome of learning to spell. For the research paper in American Literature and Humanities, my teacher explicitly taught me that writing a research paper was simply writing a five-paragraph essay and expanding the supporting arguments themselves into five-paragraph essays. (Talk about a written fractal!)

Though all these systems were just expansions on previous methods, I still found more tribulations when trying to complete the next step. Writing became more than just the ability to spell words, but rather the ability to use them to convey a pertinent message. Suffice it to say, I abhorred the entire process. Writing a loquacious paragraph—not to mention a 10,000 word paper—required hours of contemplation and drudgery. The link to Thesaurus.com became my most-frequented bookmark. The night before my research paper in American Literature was due, I stared blankly at the screen for twenty minutes before comprehending that I simply couldn't edit it anymore. I had combed through the lines so many times that I believed every word inarticulate. Nonetheless, it fit within the structure of an extensive paragraph.

Then I took AP Literature and Composition; I consider it the turning point in my writing experience. Our teacher, Mr. Demaret, never seemed to teach in a pedantic manner. For example, on the day we talked about the existentialism in Kafka's *Metamorphosis*, he flipped all the chairs upside down and moved them to the edges of the room to give us a new perspective on the class. "Why not?" he asked, in response to our questioning glances. We sat on the carpet-covered concrete and discussed why Gregor's insect state wasn't abhorrent. Gregor found so many different perspectives when he was able to crawl on the walls of his room, which opened his mind to true happiness.

Like Gregor, we learned that every paradigm about sentences, paragraphs, and essays didn't need to be followed. I don't need to count every paragraph to make sure they contain between five and seven sentences and that every assertion is supported by at least two details. My essays can be messy and complicated; my prepositions can be ended on. I don't need to begin the essay with my given name, though I can if I so choose. I don't need to flip constantly to an online thesaurus to find words I would never use in my personal dialect. Writing is a process of learning and unlearning. Once I could handle the name, sentence, paragraph, and essay, I discovered that I could also break all the rules I learned in the process. Now that I know the rules, I can choose the most effective ones to convey my message in the same way that I can sign my real or nickname depending on the tone or context. My parents, in addressing me by my nickname first, taught me that formalized systems aren't the only methods.

In college, I began first semester continuing this mentality, though my writing pursuits still largely reflect my first endeavor in spelling. When I sat down to write my first paper for my RAP class, I started a week and a half before the other students in my hall and finished just a day before them. My friends watched movies in other rooms, talked until the early morning, and spent hours debating who the best Disney princess was. Meanwhile, I listened to the satisfying click of the keys while brainstorming intricate ways to describe my thesis. I wanted to join the other students, but a premature satisfaction kept me too smug to abandon my paper for procrastination. I was satisfied with myself for sitting down to write the paper—even without parents breathing down my neck about it—while my friends procrastinated. In my mind, the more time one invested in a paper, the higher quality it would become. (This was based upon the same principal that good cheese was formed only after enzymes ruthlessly picked at the milk.) My roommate started the night before, the day after I finished editing. Surely, I believed, my work had rendered a superior paper (or at least it would taste better).

I cultivated this superiority for two weeks. When our professor handed back her graded final copy, my frustration overwhelmed me. If it took me over a week to receive a B in college, how could I possibly spend the appropriate amount of time to garner an A? She handed out the prompts only two weeks in advance, after all. We compared our grades over dinner; even the guy who began the midnight before the paper was due received a better grade than I did. How was this possible?

The smugness I felt quickly dissipated. I visited my professor later, who told me I was too ambitious in my thesis. College-level 'A' papers weren't always the ones to search too hard for an answer, but rather reach a well-supported, self-standing conclusion. My conclusion didn't succeed because I tried to cover too much material in three pages, frustrated myself, and could no longer edit it.

I often wonder why other people didn't have to spell their names with a fork at dinner, why they can write an essay in six hours that contains fewer mistakes than the one I wrote and re-wrote in nine days. But other people don't write the same way as I do; writing is an intrinsic practice that requires more time from me than others. I'm never been satisfied with one word when another elusively tickled my memory. I also want to address too many points and frustrate myself too much to continue working. This often causes me to burn out on papers, refusing to work on them after a certain amount of time. My classmates, in comparison, understand how to choose a thesis that matches their page limit. Comparing your writing process with others' is like comparing names. The more you wish you didn't need additional time to practice something so fundamental, the more frustrated you become. Just because my roommate earns better grades than I do on papers doesn't mean that my writing falls lower on a hierarchical scale. That's a childish belief; she likely has problems in areas that I excel at. Writing is personal, much like a name. I should only compare my writing to my best, not the work of others.

Personally

PAT McDONOUGH

Pat McDonough enters College Writing *with low expectations for the course, but he is almost immediately surprised to learn how different its methods and goals are from his past experiences. The rhetorical choices he makes in creating his "Writer's Statement" illustrate many of the goals of the course, and he helps readers understand both the atmosphere of the class and its assignments using quotes from his own unit essays.*

My name. That is all you know about me, reader. In fact, I am willing to bet that many of you completely ignored my name and just began reading. You don't know what I look like, where I grew up, or what I do when I'm not writing essays. You don't know that as I write this I am lying in bed in my dorm room in my pajamas, listening to Weezer while trying not to wake my roommate. Unfortunately, my name is the least important and least interesting thing about me. In order to keep you, a complete stranger, invested in what I have to say, I must establish my own personal voice through unique language and perhaps a few personal anecdotes.

On the first day of class, I stumbled into the room after everyone else and took a seat in the back. I had taken several writing classes in high school, and this one was not going to be any different, or so I decided. We were going to talk about using more sophisticated language in our essays, and maybe about how to form a persuasive argument. In essence, everything I had been learning about writing since the sixth grade. I had taken this exact class—or a close variation of it—so many times now that I wouldn't need to pay attention. Then, the teacher asked us to take out our laptops.

This, too, I had been expecting. We were going to be asked to write a brief journal entry or "all about me" piece as an icebreaker to get to know everyone. That was when we were told to open Facebook and look up our most recent status update. I obliged, wondering where he was going with this. I would be fine, however, as long as I didn't have to share. I was in a new place, after all, surrounded by people I'd never talked to before, and the status I had selected was somewhat odd. But there was no way that we would be asked to share something like that out loud, and if somebody did, it was not going to be me.

Of course, I was the first person asked. I paused, cringing as I reread the half-sentence spread out over my Facebook page. The fact that I had updated my status about the season finale of my favorite TV show now seemed incredibly nerdy. I took a deep breath, and conjured up as much courage as I could. Loudly, I read, "Dude, Breaking Bad, I'm gonna die." There were a few chuckles from around the room, but nothing as bad as I had thought. The teacher began explaining how we use different terminology and writing styles in different contexts, based on our audience, and that I likely would never have written that status that way if I had known I would be sharing it with the class. Or for that matter, if I was going to talk about the show, say, to my parents. It is important to know your audience and to write to them so they can receive the thought you are presenting for their consideration.

Sharing our work turned out to be a big part of the class. Most of it took the form of peer reviews; we would trade our essays with another member in our group to give and receive feedback. I was truly thankful for these exercises. It gave me a break from looking at my own work and see the same topic through someone else's point of view. Because we swapped essays with the same group of people every time, we were able to get comfortable with each other and give constructive criticism instead of incessantly complimenting each other's writing. Responding to questions such as ""How can the essay be extended?" or "What specific areas of the essay did you connect to as a reader?" as part of our peer feedback compelled us to read and respond critically and thoughtfully. But sharing peer feedback was not the only instance of sharing our work with our classmates.

I was a gymnast in high school. Somehow I was allowed to compete in the meets as a freshman, unlike some of my teammates. The first time I competed, I was very nervous. I had been practicing all season and now I finally had a chance to show off what I had worked for all season. I hopped up to the pommel horse and began my routine. About halfway through I missed one of my moves and ended up in the wrong position. Under the pressure of having my team, my parents, my coach, and the judge all watching me, I had messed up. I did the only thing I could: I made up the rest of my routine on the spot. It was quite clear that the judge had noticed my mistake and docked points accordingly, but at least I finished my routine without crying and running out of the gymnasium. Similar occurrences happened over the next four years, but I usually managed to keep my cool and at least finish my routine.

In my *College Writing* class I was faced with my biggest fear: presentations. We would get into our peer groups and be asked to respond to a music video or movie clip, connecting it to a composition concept we had learned, such as specificity of details, or to an essay we were reading, like Sontag's essay on war photography. My group and I would try to use all of the time given to us in order to come up with the best responses we could. Despite all of the preparation, in the beginning of the semester I would occasionally forget what I was going to say and start stammering. But then I would remember gymnastics, and how I would be able to rectify a mistake with a little bit of confidence. I was able to do the same in my presentations, and towards the middle of the semester, with the presentation being a regular feature of my class, I eventually stopped forgetting my thoughts and would not stammer anymore. Presentation and public speaking are skills that will always be very prevalent in the business world, the space I hope to work in when I graduate. So I am lucky to have learned to master them.

We learned skills that were tangible and that we could use beyond our classroom. For example, one assignment involved looking at photographs:

> In the photos of Ron Haviv, it is clear that he keeps this in mind when reporting on events. One of his most famous photos is of Guillermo Ford, the former Vice President of Panama. In 1989 Ford was attacked by a hired thug after a rally in his support. The image shows the two men in a standoff, with the attacker brandishing a weapon and Ford drenched in blood. The color of the photo is loud and chaotic, an action shot that calls attention to itself. The attacker's right arm and weapon is blurred in motion, moving in on Ford, who appears to be giving off a rather submissive gesture. The amount of action in the photo is enough to generate a surge of adrenaline, with the viewer wondering what happened.

While helping us observe the relationship between art and journalism, the assignment was also an exercise in articulating analysis. We learned how to figure out the objective of the photographers and what their pictures meant in context. Analysis is a very important ability in real life because it helps us to understand the things that surround us. In order to properly communicate with others, we must be able to understand what they mean. Helping others to understand us is also an important technique, and attention to detail is the best way of doing so. Our first essay had us writing about our homes:

> My town is in the middle of a forest. The omnipresent trees made me feel small. After many years, you got used to seeing the changes from the brown and red of the autumn to the bare snow-covered branches of the winter, the small buds in the spring. Being used to these giant beings did not make me comfortable with them, however. They often blotted out the

sun, forcing any life that lived below to live in their shadows. The trees held secrets, and during the dead of night on calm summer nights you could hear them whisper to one another. For those few short, hot weeks I could fit in. Gazing over the ocean, with the pungent marsh air pushing my hair up, I found that I could see for miles in any direction.

By using descriptive language and specific detail, I was able to convey my thoughts about my hometown to the reader. Instead of simply telling how I felt, the details allowed me to show my feelings. While the readers might not feel the same way I do about the forest or the beach, the detailed descriptions I gave of each are enough to simulate the same thoughts for them. Specificity and attention to detail can make writing relatable, even if the reader does not agree with every word.

One of the last (and one of the best) assignments in the class involved writing about our favorite genre of music and the artists within that genre. We used both our analytic skills and attention to detail to craft a personal and meaningful piece:

The song that can send me back to 1999 immediately is "The Sidewinder Sleeps Tonite," by R.E.M. It starts off with an upbeat guitar and steady drums, with the lead singer coming in with a falsetto imitation of The Tokens' "The Lion Sleeps Tonight," in what is a clear homage to the track. With those first four notes, I am always catapulted back in time. When I was little, my mother would do what she called "spring cleaning." It was essentially the same as what everyone else calls spring cleaning, except she did it around once a month, the whole year round. Every time she decided to clean the house from top to bottom, she would dig through her CD collection. (My mother is an avid fan of any and all kinds of music. Except gangsta rap.) Half of the time she would pull out R.E.M.'s *Automatic for the People* and pop it into the stereo. Cleaning the house was her way of clearing her head, and the music relieved her stress as well as made the floor-to-ceiling scrub downs less abysmally dull.

Writing about music provided excitement as well as a challenge. We had to find a way to express the emotions we associated with our beloved music. I realized that the only way to accurately portray these songs was to dive in headfirst and show the readers my personal thoughts. By putting myself in the spotlight, sharing stories and feelings, I easily captured the essence of the music that I had been listening to my entire life. While showing how I actually felt was a bit tough at first, it definitely paid off in my writing.

Adrien Brody plays an English teacher in *Detachment*. He points out the perils of constantly consuming visual media. If the images are constantly supplied, we never use our imagination. In order to stir our own imaginations, we must read, he says, for reading enables us to create our own images. We live in a world where the visual constantly surrounds us: iPods we stare at when walking across campus, the video games we play, the TV shows and movies we watch. So this class was a welcome challenge and an important learning experience. The multiple exercises in this class, on specificity of detail, on taking analysis another level deeper, and on responding to non-textual media with a written response helped me not only stir my own imagination but also articulate my imagination while bearing my audience in mind.

My experiences with the class far exceeded my expectations. I will always remember it as my first college course, but it was also more than that. We formed a sort of community in that room, joking around and engaging in the friendly competition between groups. It was the only class I looked forward to every day. I am sad to see it go, but I know that the friends I made and the techniques I learned will stay with me.

Finding Peace—The Intimate Experience of Writing

PETER WHITE

In his "Writer's Statement," Peter White moves between discussing his work on particular assignments and delving into his personal context. He has discovered that the act of writing itself can create for him what he calls "pockets of air" in the midst of an era filled with endless distractions. And these "pockets" allow him to use writing for many purposes: to learn, to discover, to heal, and to face and change uncomfortable facts about himself.

The human mind has a fascinating and mysterious strength in us all. It is the "key" to life that makes us individual from the rest of the world. Through the many powerful feelings and thoughts in each of us, the mind and all that we experience help shape us into who we are. They are a part of our greater story, subconsciously helping make decisions for us every day. However, without a method of channeling, processing, and understanding our thoughts and feelings, we can quickly lose sight of who we are, what our purpose is, and how to become the best we can be. There are many practices to help center the mind, but not all methods work for everyone because each of us is uniquely different from everyone else. For me, I found peace and continue to find peace through writing. What follows is a small telling of the journey I have taken to get where I am today. I have not fully reached my destination, but I have crossed a milestone that has helped me to begin understanding who I am and the many blessings I am privileged to have.

* * *

At the time I was applying to attend a university, I thought college was not for me. I had learned to be a skilled carpenter and have sold the pieces of furniture I make for thousands of dollars. If I really wanted to, I could make a living with my abilities. But during my senior year in high school, I didn't feel ready to commit to college, and I didn't think I would find satisfaction in becoming a furniture maker. I decided to defer my admission and see what the world had to offer me, to see if I could find answers to questions that had plagued me for years. I was a painfully shy individual during my first three years of high school, but I never wanted to be. I felt stuck and questioned my worth even though I had many friends who loved me. Even with my best friends, I would often look at the floor instead of at them as they said hi to me in the halls. In hopes of finding myself, of coming to peace with who I am, I took a job as a full time supervisor to six sub-contractors—a stimulating and multi-faceted job. I was paid handsomely, my work was both efficient and organized, and my supervisor and colleagues welcomed and appreciated me. Despite all of this apparent success, I was still no closer to finding contentment or peace with who I am... until one day I was challenged by a UMass professor to express myself through pen and paper.

* * *

Coming to UMass has been one of the most wonderful challenges I have ever faced, but frankly, there was one challenge I believed I could live without. When I attended New Student Orientation in June before my freshman year and signed up for ENGLWRIT 112, I was very nervous. I had always hated writing, and I knew in my gut that I was going to hate the course. I believed papers were a waste of time, and an entire course dedicated to essay development and revisions would be even more so. But a lot of things happened during this course that proved me wrong. In fact, I have never been more wrong about something in my life.

* * *

I believe that for the majority of people, the most difficult battles we experience in life are the ones we have within ourselves, and it is easy to avoid fighting them in an age where distraction is so readily available. In order to find peace, it is essential for an individual to find a way to overcome these inward battles. We need to find what I think of as "pockets of air" in each day to allow us to process things in our lives rather than to fill them with distractions. I fell victim to this avoidance, and as a result, finding peace with who I am became my greatest conflict yet. Although life at UMass has greatly helped me find my peace, I have found the majority of my peace through writing.

* * *

Beginning with the first unit of my *College Writing* class, I struggled greatly to understand how to talk about myself. It was not something I had ever practiced, and it made me very uncomfortable. In this essay, I relived a moment in time on my Great-grandfather's farm that has influenced me my entire life:

As my Great-grandfather (Bumpa as I called him) was preparing the tractor so I could drive it, a gift for my sixth birthday, he simply asked me what I wanted to do in life. At six years old, I had never really given much thought to this question; I never felt a serious response was necessary at the time. With Bumpa, however, it was different. Although we spent a lot of time together, he was never a man of many words, and when he spoke, it was with intention and purpose. So I thought about the question while he opened up the hood of the tractor to pour diesel into the tank. When he finished, I remember stating with certainty that I wanted to be a worker man like him. This made him laugh out loud and his response was "Then you will be."

I always knew his words "Then you will be" had a great impact on me, but until this assignment, I had never forced myself to truly consider what these words meant to me. I experienced great enlightenment in this unit because it taught me the power writing can have on an individual. Words greatly influence the impact that a story will have on an audience, and word choice needs to change accordingly depending on the intended audience and purpose of the essay. Learning how to "show" a moment, as opposed to "telling" a moment invites the reader to experience the emotions the author has intended to share. I "show" my Great-grandfather in the final product of my essay:

> His laugh was thunderous as he caught each of my siblings and me, and his hugs were the same as always: warm, powerful, and comforting. He could throw each of us very high with little effort, and despite my fear of heights, I was okay with him doing so because I trusted him like no one else. His hands were rough and calloused from the continuous turning of the soil in his fields, and his clothes were neat but stained from the dirt and grease acquired whenever he did maintenance on his tractor.

This "shows" my Great-grandfather because from this excerpt, you can interpret a kind, strong, warm, hard-working man. I could have simply "told" the reader all this, but by "showing" him, I have invited the reader to interpret the story on his or her own. The overall experience is more comfortable and effective for the reader, and as the writer, it was my first step into understanding writing as a way of processing my thinking.

* * *

In the second unit, I learned how to analyze and interpret a text. This was also something I was terrible at. In my entire life, I can confidently say I have read fewer than fifty books and for any argumentative essay, I have always fallen asleep before finishing it. That was up until this unit. Through the intimate discussions in class and with my professor in conferences, I came to appreciate the many different ways an essay can be interpreted. I had never considered the idea that everyone reads and interprets essays differently. I now realize that our own context and life stories greatly influence everything we read, say, and do. And so it is incredibly important that we learn how to understand our own individual context as well as attempting to make contact with both the context of the essay's author and our intended audience. This understanding prompted the topic for my second essay when I read "Is Google Making Us Stupid?" by Nicholas Carr. Upon reading his text about technology and how it is affecting our mental abilities, I challenged his idea and took his work a step further by making observations as to how technology is making us numb. My intention was to encourage my readers to allow less distraction into their lives, enabling them to find the "pockets" I previously mentioned.

Peer responses were very helpful to me in Unit Two because they helped teach me how to write a persuasive argument for my audience. My class had many different personalities, and this allowed me to adapt my essay to reach out to as many different people as I was able. Mostly, my revisions came from the questions my peers asked me during conversations I had with them. They would make statements like "I don't fully understand what you mean by this accusation you are making" and "What advice would you give to help people put down their phones?" These sorts of interactions taught me to consider potential questions readers may have from reading my texts and to answer them before they are asked. Accomplishing this, however, will always require a lot of advice from colleagues and a lot of revision if I am to most success-fully deliver my purpose.

* * *

Revision is the most intimate part of writing; it is when the author needs to test his own work and consider new words, styles, ideas, and methods to most efficiently communicate his ideas. Every essay during my course underwent extensive revisions at least twice, for example, my fourth unit. The goal of this unit was to revise a previous essay for a new audience, with a new purpose, form, and voice. I decided to revise my first essay by writing a letter to my Great-grandfather who had passed away over eight years ago. This was a great trial for me. I hadn't spoken to him since I had prayed to him at his funeral. To share my feelings with him in 1200 words or less was difficult, but this required me to consider what I most wanted him to know about me today. If I hadn't revised my initial draft, where I talked about the weather at his funeral, I would have regretted not telling him how the four words "Then you will be" have shaped me into the man I am today. It's amazing the level of impact a moment can have on a person. With that sentence, one of the most influen-tial men I have ever met built the foundation of the work ethic I have today. If I want to accomplish a goal, I will as long as I go into it with an open and persistent mind. Applying these ethics to writing, I feel more accomplished because of my revisions. In order to successfully achieve revision, you must completely open your mind to understand your own work in a new light. You need to become your audience and answer as many questions as you can. It is very difficult for people to relate to one another unless minds are open and accepting of new ideas. For me, revision became a kind of meditation. I was required to unclutter my mind of all the noise that it is so easily filled with, and create a channel for fresh virgin thoughts to flow. Subsequently, revision brought me one step closer to finding peace within myself.

* * *

Writing is a truly intimate experience. It requires a lot of time and patience, but it will never stop helping you if you take the proper steps to nurture and develop it. I came into this course despising writing, and I now leave this course with a love for writing. My advice to you is this: allow yourself to fall victim to this remarkably enlightening process. I challenge you to expand what you learn in this course and to apply it to every aspect of your life. Use writing to explore your ideas; to channel your thoughts and feelings; and to understand your disappointments, your goals, and your identity. We all have our strengths and weaknesses, but it isn't impossible to harvest our weaknesses and make them stronger. Every time I confront my discomforts through writing, I become more comfortable with them. You can never stop growing if you push yourself. Use this course as a milestone to help you achieve greater than your best. It will be challenging and it will require a lot of time, but in the end, I promise, you will find that you are not only a better writer, but also a well-spoken individual with a voice to be heard. I found my peace in writing. You may not, but I know either way you will greatly benefit if you engage in this experience.

I Know the Secret: An Ars Poetica

MARISSA WILKINSON

Marissa Wilkinson focuses her "Writer's Statement" on the "secret of writing" that has eluded her throughout her past English classes—until now. Through her College Writing course, she has learned about both the power of the writer and the power of the reader. As the writer, she has the power to manipulate language and form to attempt to precisely convey her meaning. But she also learns that there is a constant flow of creation and re-creation between the writer and the reader.

I used to wonder if English teachers possessed "the secret of writing." They always seemed to know the "correct" interpretation behind a piece of literature and could pull insightful thoughts out of language. I wondered if there was some aspect of writing I did not understand.

I love writing, or at least the idea of writing. Whenever a thought pops into my mind, I rush to jot it down. I could pen an epic poem, a best-selling novel, or an award winning essay with one of my ideas. I love picturing you, the reader, nodding and following along with my images and interpretations. I used to think that with my mind, pen, and paper, I could control what you thought and felt.

My *College Writing* class identified what I was feeling as the *power* of writing. Writing can be influential, as evidenced through the novels and essays whose ideas have transcended time. However, this "power" is not one-way. A constant flow of power moves between a writer and their readers.

Of course, writing would not physically exist without a writer. Right now, I am arranging words in a way that communicates my "big idea" most effectively. This ability is the writer's power over language, most strongly illustrated through the concept my instructor referred to as "Breaking English" and language in general. I define languages as sets of rules used to guide my reader to a certain feeling or thought. I can choose to break these rules of proper grammar and language if that is what it takes to portray my idea accurately. When English is broken and language loses rules, an endless stream of meaning and new knowledge begins. I assert power by breaking language to fit my ideas. My ideas cannot always be conveyed through traditional, standard patterns and phrases. During the research paper, we focused on "showing, not telling," another instance of a writer's power. Language can form simple statements or describe details vividly. To be a more powerful writer, I had to learn to *show* you what I meant, not just *tell* you. By asserting my power over language, I affirm the strength and value of my ideas. My thoughts don't have to be compromised or categorized by language—unless I want that. I can make language compromise for me.

Having power over language puts me, the writer, in a position of leadership. When writing an anecdote, I exhibit personal leadership by molding language to fit a specific context, but I also exhibit public leadership. I have the power of language, but the responsibility of keeping you, my audience, captivated through it.

The "secret" I could never understand before this class is the unrecognized power that the READER possesses. While I as writer retain the power of language and personal opinion, you the reader hold the power of interpretation. You can respond to the meanings and ideas I present in my writing. The typical academic paper, your first assignment, is the simplest and most direct method of response. Responding can mean agreeing, disagreeing, contending, expanding—however you think your reaction will be accurately documented. You have the power of your own opinion, and the power to make something new from my writing.

Teachers and other readers are responders like you, and the "secret" is your power. You can interpret writing to whatever you believe the meaning is as long as you can back up your opinion. You can create your own meaning.

Before this class, I never realized the constant power balance between you and me, the reader and writer. We share the power of creating new meaning and knowledge. A piece of writing contains power from both the physical words and the intangible ideas. My idea is a piece of new knowledge or understanding, and your interpretation adds more new meaning to the knowledge. An endless cycle of knowledge building flows between us. You become the writer when you respond, thus continuing the cycle.

Through group discussions and constant introspection in this class, I have learned the "secret." I understand the power of language I possess as a writer, and the simultaneous power of interpretation I possess as a reader. Because I can function as both reader and writer, the cycle of meaning and creating knowledge flows through me personally. The cycle also connects me to every other writer and reader out there. Including you.

Tell me, reader: how do you feel? Respond, for I have learned the secret. Use this class wisely, and you may know it for yourself.